Prais

Get Out! Every Student Pastor on the planet knows it should be a defining reality of their ministry, yet so few actually execute it. Being with people is not a ministry strategy, it's an implication of the gospel itself. *Get Out* offers Student Pastors a theological framework and some very helpful ideas on getting out of your office and meeting students where they are. Buy a couple copies of this book; one for yourself and one for another Student Pastor.

Jason Gaston
Student Pastor
The Summit Church, RDU, North Carolina

There is not a book that Dr. Alvin Reid has written that I have not read. Every one of them has pushed and challenged me as a leader and minister. *Get Out*, once again, is a must read. I have always said, "If you ain't amongst 'em, you ain't reaching 'em." This father and son book gives you the practical on the why and how of getting "amongst 'em." I believe every one in ministry should pick this book up and read it, no matter if you do Sr Adult ministry, Pre School Ministry or anywhere in-between. Once read, you will have a clear understanding of what it takes to be a minister TO your community, not just in your community.

Brian Mills
Executive Teaching/Ministries Pastor
Englewood Baptist Church, Jackson, Tennessee

The first sentence on the first page of the introduction is all it took to hook me because of an identical experience which left in an indelible mark on my own parenting practices! A very powerful and convincing package...a book on missional student ministry by the "Prof" of millennial missional living matched with his millennially-focused son who currently serves as a Student Ministry Pastor! Because of this profound pairing this book is a marvelous blend of the practical and the theoretical, featuring real-time examples from seasoned Student Ministry veterans who are "getting out" of the church campus to the school campus and community!

Victor Flores
Pastor of Student Ministries
Bell Shoals Baptist Church, Brandon, Florida

Packed with practical insight and ministry suggestions, the reader will be tempted to bypass the foundational principles that the authors build upon and jump right to experimentation with new ideas. The practical helps come from years of combined ministry experiences and the unique father-son perspective that is grounded in a commitment to disciple making that began at home. Alvin and Josh wisely provide a biblical and historical context that begins with prayer and the centrality of the gospel and calls the reader to embrace the missionary call to *Get Out*. Combining years of ministry and life experience while also calling on veteran youth ministry practitioners, Alvin and Josh provide a biblical and historical context for an "out of the church building---into the community" understanding of student ministry. Their unique father-son perspective is grounded in a commitment to disciple making that began at home. Now, this experience provides foundational and practical insight for all who resonate with the call to *Get Out* and make disciples of the next generation in any setting.

Matthew D. Kearns, Dmin
Leadership Development Team Leader,
Missouri Baptist Convention, SBC

Get Out is an incredible resource that every student pastor and volunteer should read. The book gives great examples from scripture and testimonies of student guys who are engaged in mission which make this book a powerful resource. Alvin and Josh also lay out a clear strategy for engaging leaders and students to be mission immediately. Pick up a copy for you and a student ministry friend!

Jeff Borton
Student Pastor
Christ Fellowship Church, Miami, Florida

GET OUT

Student Ministry
in the Real World

**Alvin L. Reid
and Josh Reid**

Get Out
Student Ministry in the Real World

Published by Rainer Publishing
www.rainerpublishing.com

ISBN 978-0692350959

Printed in the United States of America

Contents

FOREWORD

In today's church there is a multiplicity of student ministry philosophies and methodologies. They are all striving towards what they perceive to be healthy ministry for a certain population of people typically between the sixth or seventh grade and the twelfth grade. This is a massive undertaking for any leader(s) regardless of education, preparation, or prior experience. After all a young lady who is a sophomore in high school has very little in common with a male eighth-grader, even though the two are separated by only a couple of years. Furthermore, as a student journey's the vast terrain of middle then high school their bodies and minds will undergo more change than any other time throughout their life. Throw into this mix a world that is spinning so fast it feels like we are looking at the future in retrospect, and the role or task of the student pastor becomes all the more complicated and valued. Unsurprisingly the arena of student ministry has become busier with competing ideas on how to better accomplish the task of student ministry.

It is into this arena that my friend, and former professor, Dr. Alvin Reid, along with his son Josh Reid, addresses what should be an indispensible aspect for every student ministry. Dr. Reid has been a keen observer of student ministry for nearly twenty-five years and has afforded Josh a front row seat and back stage pass to many styles and approaches to ministry through the years. Additionally Josh has served on staff under the leadership of Matt Lawson, an incredible and respected student pastor, at First Baptist Church Woodstock. As I read the following pages it is obvious the additional impact that Matt had on Josh's thinking.

In *Get Out: Student Ministry in the Real World* these men sound the alarm on what should be essential for any ministry, regardless of philosophy or methodology. Every student ministry should have an ongoing presence outside of the church where the daily comings and goings of student life take place. In many ways this book exists to guard the student pastor's thinking from excuses and serve as a catalyst for ways of engagement. Alvin and Josh write with a healthy underlying assumption, one cannot follow Jesus in leading a ministry and never stand at the crossroads where culture intersects with a teenager. If you agree with this assumption then the following pages will serve you well. *Get Out* will serve as a resource on your shelf you return to over and over to prime the pump on ways to engage. The authors have success-fully provided us a simple roadmap and collection of practical helps affording the leader to be more Great Commission focused.

Alvin and Josh orbit around the central idea of this book offering readers a perspective from one who is seasoned and one at the beginning of a season. Both men believe in a standard of excellence:

- When a student arrives on a church campus for midweek service or Sunday morning small groups...
- That camps and retreats atmosphere's should be bathed in prayer and rich with preparation...
- And that mission trips to far off distant lands can and should leave an indelible impact on a student's worldview...

Yet while we build programs, strategize events, and prepare mission trips, the mission of God calls us and causes us to deeper waters. A ministry with the heart to engage is one that desires influence beyond Sunday services, because they are helping students to be missionaries in the here and now. After reading this book, the question we all must answer is, are we willing to *Get Out*?!

Brent Crowe, PhD
Vice President, Student Leadership University,
Orlando, Florida

INTRODUCTION:
It's Time to Get Out

Of all the advice I (Alvin) got as a parent, the best I have ever received--and the advice I pass on the most--is this: find what your kids love to do and do it with them. Both Josh and I love sports. Beginning with a trip to Wrigley Field when Josh was 12, we have been to over ten different Major League Baseball parks. We've enjoyed live NFL and NBA games, more than a few trips to see our local Durham Bulls baseball team, and more Tar Heel games--football, basketball, and baseball--than we can remember. I helped coach Josh when he played soccer, basketball, and football. We love sports and have enjoyed watching them whether live or on TV.

As Josh grew both spiritually and physically, he became an accomplished drummer. I believe in helping students involved in ministry earlier rather than later, starting with our own children. So, Josh began traveling with me in a worship band from his freshman year in high school through college. We learned that doing things we love--whether as the dad or the son--can include things that matter for eternity, like ministering to young people at camps, D-Nows, and rallies.

Today, Josh is a youth pastor, and I am just about the oldest youth speaker going. I have written a lot of books on a variety of topics over the years, but nothing excites me more than writing this book with my son. God has graciously grown us both to serve Christ together.

Back to the earlier discussion about sports: one thing that drives us crazy is so-called "prevent" defenses. This is the defensive posture taken by a team in the lead so as not to lose the advantage. The problem with a prevent defense is it shifts from an aggressive, attack mentality to a more passive, don't-screw-up posture. Too many times a prevent defense actually prevents a team from winning! Just this week I watched an NFL team lose a game in the final seconds because they nursed a slim lead with a "prevent" mentality. Once you lose the momentum it's really hard to get it back. The teams that demonstrate a perennial proclivity toward winning tend to be those that never take their foot off the gas pedal when they have a lead.

We fear that the same problem seen in prevent defenses can be applied to a lot of student ministry today. Without intending to do so, so much of student ministry––and many Christian parents––focus so much on protecting teens from the evil around us that they create a safety-first, hold-the-fort mentality. There is plenty of evil around us, make no mistake about that! The problem is this attitude happens at the time when young people exhibit a greater interest in exploring, learning, and taking risks. When the church sends a message of protection over mission, young people inevitably find some place to explore. Often these places are the very environments the church seeks to protect them from.

We believe a successful sports team must pursue winning and create a culture that focuses on doing what matters to make winning a habit. To quote a former NFL coach, "We play to win the game." Much more importantly, we believe that focusing students and their families—and the entire student ministry—on aggressively reaching out to touch and love others, is at the same time the best way to protect them from evil and to grow their faith. A great affection for Christ and a radical obedience to Christ leaves little time to waste one's life. Give students a mission, keep them focused, and they don't have time to focus on the evil around them. We think Jesus would agree, for the last thing He told His followers to do was quite an aggressive and ambitious goal: to go and make disciples of all the nations. He said it in different ways in each Gospel and in the Acts:

- "Go, make disciples of all peoples" (Matthew 28:19)
- "Go into all the world and proclaim the gospel" (Mark 16:15)
- "Repentance and forgiveness of sins should be proclaimed to all nations" (Luke 24:47)
- "As the Father sent me, so I send you" (John 20:21)
- "You will receive power when the Holy Spirit comes upon you, and you will be My witnesses in Jerusalem, Judea, Samaria, and the ends of the earth" (Acts 1:8)

In this book we argue that the more we can shift from a youth *group* (inward, me-focused) to a student *ministry* (outward, Jesus-focused), two things happen: one, we will reach more people; but also, our students will experience stronger spiritual growth. And a residual impact will be young people avoiding the world, the flesh, and the devil as they seek to restore our world through the gospel.

> A great affection *for* Christ and a radical obedience *to* Christ leaves little time to *waste* one's life.

This book serves as a primer on student ministry focused specifically on getting out of the church building into the community to impact it for Christ. It is not intended to be a complete book on student ministry in general or on missional student ministry in particular. I attempted to do that in my book *As You Go: Creating a Missional Culture of Gospel-Centered Students.* This book builds on that one with practical helps for student pastors, parents, and students to be effective outside the church building in the culture, in particular the public school.

Don't misunderstand us; we see great biblical value in gathering the church for corporate worship, for student pastors and other ministers having office hours and being engaged with other ministries in the church, and for attractional evangelistic efforts. It's not either-or; it is both-and. But we feel the correction needed in student ministry is to shift to a more Great

Commission focus than a fortress mentality, for the church is less a hotel for saints than it is a hospital for sinners. We encounter a lot of student pastors who feel that way as well.

The Western Church faces a significant change in culture in our time. Student ministry is in the heart of the vortex of change. "The combined impact of the Information Age, postmodern thought, globalization, and racial-ethnic pluralism that has seen the demise of the grand American story also has displaced the historic role the church has played in that story," Researcher Mike Regele observed, continuing: "As a result, we are seeing the marginalization of the institutional church."[1] Just because your student ministry has been effective in the past featuring events and personalities does not mean it stands ready to face the challenges to the gospel in our time.

Christianity in the West has been increasingly marginalized in our culture; many of us simply refuse to see it. We certainly have not lost all our influence, but on many issues that were once in the center of American society (protecting the unborn; the sanctity of marriage; heterosexual marriage only; to name a few) have now been pushed out of the mainstream of cultural norms. How do we respond? We must think less like Christians enjoying a home field advantage and more like Christians living as missionaries. In their excellent book *Everyday Church*, Chester and Timmis argue for a shift in ministry focus to meet the challenges of our time, and this shift especially relates to the front line of student ministry: *"Our marginal status is an opportunity to rediscover the missionary call of the people of God.* We can recover witness to Christ unmuddied by nominal Christianity."[2]

Recently I spoke to a group of student ministry leaders near Atlanta. A lady talked to me about her role leading a pregnancy support center in her town. She has open access to public schools to talk about sex education and has some freedom to involve student pastors with her work. But, she tells me, student pastors she knows have such an expectation of being at the church building that they cannot easily get to the school to help her. No doubt there are student pastors who do not value such a ministry. But when real student pastors who truly want to help, but cannot because of the expectation of their overseers to be in the church building is to the point they cannot help at the school, we need to rethink what we are doing.

If you agree that we are in need of a renewed focus in student ministry where we increasingly center much of what we do off the church campus and into our communities, read on. You will encounter testimonies from a number of student pastors who will help you navigate these unstable waters. One of these is Spencer Barnard. Spencer observed firsthand the change in so many communities in our day and how they impact our ministries:[3]

I'm the lead student pastor at The Church at Battle in Tulsa, Oklahoma. Campus ministry is a huge part of what we do on all of our campuses. In my 16 years of doing student ministry my strategy has changed a lot. Just in the last five years things have drastically changed. The days of showing up at lunch with pizza for students are over in most places. You have to earn the right to be on a campus. There needs to be a reason for you to be on a campus. Where a lot of student pastors go wrong is that we show up and say we are there to hang out with students. We could do that in the past, but when 30-year-olds or even 20-year-olds show up on a junior high or high school campus, it's just weird in this culture today. It worked 10 years ago, but in most places it just doesn't work anymore. There needs to be a reason we are there: we should be there to serve and support the administration. Our role is to be there for the school, and not to expect the school to be there for us. With that in mind we have to be careful to follow all the school's rules and present ourselves in a respectful way.

Here are some of the ways we serve schools:

- *We take food to the teacher's lounges and teacher in-service days. One of the best things that has happened for us is the government cutting funds for the schools, because it gave us the opportunity to meet their needs first hand.*

- *We make our facilities available to them for meetings and banquets. We hosted 10 different sporting banquets this last year and it has earned us a great reputation with our schools and also showcased our facilities to students and parents.*

- *We talk with coaches and teachers about leadership training or becoming chaplains for sporting teams. We found out that many coaches loved the extra help.*

- *We take drinks to the band, cheerleaders, and sporting teams.*

- *We are on the substitute teacher list. Also, some schools need volunteers to monitor testing.*

We have learned that students need to see that we have a reason for being on that campus. We get a lot more validity by getting the administration's blessing. Then students will trust our team a lot quicker. Getting to know the principal and the office staff has been huge as well. We will take with us some Starbucks' gift cards or Chick-Fil-a cards to give away as we meet teachers, coaches or administration. I actually created a position specifically aimed at connecting us to coaches and faculty of the junior high and high schools in our area. He also helps us set up events for schools such as banquets, and meeting in our building. The final thing we do, and probably one of the biggest connecting points for us with schools, is FCA (Fellowship of Christian Athletes). FCA has a great reputation on all of our campuses. We have developed a great relationship with them and, because of it, they have allowed our staff to become huddle leaders at eight different campuses around our city. This gives us a huge opportunity to connect with students who normally don't attend church at all. We have seen our student ministry grow by about 50% over the last eight months, and I would attribute it to how our team has shifted our work regarding campus ministry.

Okay, so his church is probably bigger than yours. You likely cannot go out and hire someone the way he did. Neither can Josh nor I in our ministries (his to students, mine to young professionals). Whether you use volunteers or paid staff is not the issue, but the mindset of getting out of the church building onto the campus is critical.

Centuries ago a pastor named Richard Baxter witnessed a powerful spiritual awakening in his church and community. A central part of this movement grew out of his habit of spending two days a week from morning till dark in the community ministering and witnessing. His ministry of "getting out" led to a powerful work of God's Spirit in their church. We believe God still honors churches focused more on what they do for Christ in the community than simply doing things inside the church facility. Are you ready to GET OUT? Let's go!

CHAPTER 1

GET CLARITY:
A Clear Vision for Student Ministry

> "I have but one passion: It is He, it is He alone. The world is the field and the field is the world; and henceforth that country shall be my home where I can be most used in winning souls for Christ."— Zinzendorf

"It's 3:00 PM. Get out of here. You don't need to be in the office. Go!" If you haven't heard these words while on the job, you're probably still dreaming that you would hear them. Outside of sales calls and business trips, rarely will you hear these words while at work. You have an expected and planned agenda, a day full of phone calls, emails and meetings. The greatest moment of your day just may be that lunch break. Why? Not food. Not relaxation for half an hour. Fantasy football. A make believe, imaginary team that you're the fake coach for is the highlight of your day. The clock strikes somewhere between 12:30 and 1:00 and you're back to it: phone calls, emails, meetings, and an occasional one-on-one interview. This corporate opportunity is not nearly what it seemed it would be when you applied. If only 5:00 would get here sooner.

You read the above paragraph and you are now thinking, "I thought this book was about student ministry. I promise that's what the cover said." You're right. It is about student ministry, but what I (Josh) previously described just might sound like your church. Read it again. Sound familiar? Many churches treat staff expectations the same as in a corporate job. The only issue is this: if we were to sit at our desks on the phone all day, we would fail to do what Jesus did. We would fail to get out. We would forget to go to another place, a place where students are, namely the local schools and athletic fields. As a student pastor, your office should be mobile. You need a place to study, plan and strategize with your fellow staff members. An office functions as that place. However, students will not come to you in your office as often as you can go to them in their environment. It's time to get out, but we must obtain some clarity on why we should get out first.

People crave clarity. If clarity were not craved, then there would be no need for job interviews. Anyone could get the job with no true guidance. There would be no need for leadership because we would already know how to lead. In fact, we wouldn't need road signs, because we would already understand exactly how to drive and where to go. On the contrary, we need clarity. We desire to have a clear, focused goal or reason for doing something. With that in mind, let's look at a few road signs; clear markers that tell us to get out among our students.

Lead a Student Ministry Not a Youth Group

Student pastors who get out lead student ministries. They do not lead youth groups. You may have always thought of these as the same thing. I don't mean to rock your world, but I do want to show you a slight and significant difference between the two. A *youth group* refers to a group of teenagers who meet together most likely for the sake of worshiping Jesus. Sounds the same so far, right? When we call teenagers "youth," we have unintentionally allowed them to believe that they are children rather than teenagers getting closer to adulthood daily, which is one of the problems of contemporary ministry to students. When you call teenagers "students" that is literally what they are, with the exception of those who don't currently attend school. I would argue that even if that is the case, they are there learning about Jesus and thus are students of the Word. Let's be honest; we are all students at some point. You edify your teenagers by treating them as students rather than children.

> We need to treat teenagers like young adults moving to adulthood ready for the mission of God, not children finishing their childhood in need of babysitting.
> — Alvin Reid, *Raising the Bar.*

The second part of this terminology centers on a "group" contrasted to a "ministry." A group displays inward focus while a ministry displays outward focus. If we desire to get out, doing the work of the ministry outside of the four walls of the church, it is important to understand this contrast. Push your students to be a part of a ministry rather than a group who might meet for the purpose of making each other feel better.

Focus on advancing God's mission in our world more than maintaining the status quo of our group. Iron sharpens iron. We need to build one another up, but the reason should change. We build one another up so that we may reach our respective communities more effectively with the gospel message.

Look at the example of Jesus as the disciples experienced life with Him. They worked in ministry with our Savior, clearly far better than any pastor with whom you and I could work. Jesus ushered in a clear and simple vision in Matthew 4:18-21: "Follow me, and I will make you fishers of men" (v. 19, ESV). His calling was so simple that they immediately followed Him, leaving everything behind! Being told to go fish for people probably came off as weird, but what I notice is that Jesus did not give them a four-point message on why they need to fish for people. He would explain all that as they walked closely to Him.

What does this simple vision tell us? We need to get out of our respective offices and get into the lives of those around us. Yes, there is office work to be done; but our conversations with many student pastors reveal an admission by most that the expectation of their churches is more toward them being on the church campus than on the local school campus. There are many students without Christ who wouldn't come to our churches, but would meet us for a free lunch with their friends. We'll talk about some effective ways to get out soon, but we need to understand clearly the "get out" mentality.

You may be thinking, "That's awesome what the disciples were able to do with Jesus, but they had Jesus with them wherever they went." That's true until the ascension. Following His death and resurrection, Jesus ascended into Heaven to be with the Father until the day that He returns, which we eagerly await! Imagine how the disciples felt. Jesus walked with them daily, teaching them how to actively serve their community and then He simply left. Confusion, uncertainty, and nervousness: these things crept into their minds I'm sure. How were they to succeed in proclaiming the gospel? Better yet, how are we to do so? Jesus told us: He sent us the Spirit to guide us. The Holy Spirit moves in power daily and moved in power in biblical times. Our message is unambiguous, as it was with the disciples. Get out and make disciples (Matthew 28:19-20).

When the Holy Spirit came, the disciples were filled with great power (see Acts 2-4). The fraternity of student pastors is a strange breed. We have "outreach events" where we beg and plead God to move in power, often saying that we expect God to move during those events. I do this and I often mean it. Then the day after the event happens. We're excited about what God did and, hopefully, we begin following up with students and the decisions made.

Fast forward to the next Monday. We forgot the event happened. Why? We didn't intend for that to happen. We simply forgot that the Holy Spirit is just as powerful on Monday when no special event is happening as He is when something super awesome is on the forefront! We can't discount the power of the Holy Spirit in our ministries that we are blessed to lead. The same Holy Spirit at work in our church events is active in the local community.

Consider what the disciples did once they recognized the Spirit's coming. They got out. Jesus told them to, after all: "You will be my witnesses in Jerusalem, Judea, Samaria, and the uttermost parts of the earth" (Acts 1:8). They went into the public square, the common areas, where people lived (see Acts 5:42; 16; 17:17). This means more than the public school campus. For you, it may be the local Starbucks. It may be Wal-Mart (yes, Wal-Mart is a hangout spot for a lot of students, especially in rural settings). Too often we try to create a place for students to hangout when we should be going where they already do. One of the marks of this Millennial generation is a love for Third Places like coffee shops. We need to know those places and frequent them when students are there.

If we are going to be like the disciples, we need the hearts they had. Read Acts 19:8-10. Read how Paul and the disciples moved out of the religious establishment into the culture. We forget that we don't go to church; we are the church, whether in worship on Sunday or at a ball game on Friday. We must be a mobile church and set the tone as mobile church leaders who are willing to get uncomfortable in the area outside of our offices.

Veteran student pastor Brian Mills on his vision for student ministry: "My number one philosophy is this: to be the student minister not only to my church, but also to my community. This creates an outreach, "get out" focus that automatically gets you out of the office more than in it because you are building relationships in the community.[4]

Staying in a confined space did not advance the early missionary movements. They were advanced on mission. When we turn inwardly God will propel us outwardly or we will die. Imagine if Jesus had simply stayed in one place when He walked this earth. He raised the bar by taking a group of ordinary men and interacting with people outside of that group. Missionaries do the same. William Carey went to Burma. George Whitefield is widely known for having such a great voice that he could be heard for great distances without any amplification, given there was no amplification in that day. He traveled seven times to the American colonies to preach the gospel in the open air. David Brainerd went to the Indians. D.L. Moody preached in theaters and other "secular" venues. Billy Graham preached at a vast number of crusades throughout his life. These primarily happened in football stadiums across the country as well as many stadiums overseas. A group of young college guys prayed under a haystack in 1806; some got out of the country as a result of this "haystack revival" and led a missionary movement.

Notice that while much ministry occurred within the walls of a church, massive numbers of people have come to faith in Christ because a few men were willing to get out into the public arenas. In our context as student pastors, we see many parachurch ministries engulfing our campuses whether it is the Fellowship of

Christian Athletes, Cru, Young Life, etc. So many people are getting out; yet so few of those people appear to be student pastors.

> "Being on campus with students for a single day can accomplish what decades of youth ministry within the walls of a church cannot." — Ryan Sharp[5]

Allow me to debunk a myth that I believed until about a year ago. I knew about FCA, Young Life and Cru. I heard and experienced great things that they were doing. I have spent a great amount of time with FCA, whether speaking at local high schools or leading worship at an FCA camp over a summer. I thought that they had it covered. These leaders would take care of all the ministry needs on each campus. That's a myth. The local church can honestly meet the needs much better. Parachurch ministries are great at getting out. They can meet short-term needs. We must become available and ready to meet the long-term needs of discipleship in each student's life. It is wise to partner with these ministries. They are probably willing to partner with you, but you must be ready and willing! Live your life getting out with the truth of the gospel rather than believing the myth that others will always take care of that part of ministry.

Most Student Pastors Want to Get Out

When you accepted the call to be a pastor to students did you sign up for a desk job or a mobile job? Most student pastors I meet tell me they would love the opportunity to get out into their respective communities. The ones who are on campus throughout each week tell me that their favorite part of being a student pastor outside of seeing students come to know Christ is the opportunity to go to football practice to encourage the players or the opportunity to speak at an FCA meeting on campus. While this attitude rings true with the majority of student pastors I know, many student pastors struggle with the actual practice of getting out. As noted in the Introduction, the world has changed and schools are not as open as they were. We want to help you with that.

Maybe you're like some who would say, "Josh, I love the idea of getting on campus. I love the idea of investing in the lives of students outside of this office, but I simply don't know how." Have no fear as some practical tips are coming your way! Maybe you know how, but you don't have the favor of the local campuses in your area. After time of learning from other great student pastors, here are a few principles for starters:

1. *Before you do anything suggested in this book, you must pray.* Pray before you go. Pray as you're going. Pray when you leave. God opens up the doors that we often close because of our own spiritual stupidity. When we bathe ministry in prayer, God understands that we are not trying to do something without His help. We get out while holding His hand along the way.

2. *Follow any and all rules that the high school and middle school campuses have.* I know the visitor tags aren't hipster, but they are effective. Wearing them not only identifies you to everyone, but it also tells the office staff that you're truly there to serve them and their school. Unfortunately, some of you may not be highly favored because of other churches in the area or your predecessor's unwillingness to follow those rules.

3. *Start with the administration, getting to know the principal, receptionist, coaches, and others.* More about this later.

4. *Be involved with FCA or whatever Christian organization there is on the campus.* That's the

most welcoming environment to you as a minister in the area.

5. *Look for places you can volunteer and serve.* Much more about that in the following pages, but here are a couple of examples:

> *One way that I have been getting out into the community is by becoming an assistant coach for the high school football team. This opportunity has allowed me to speak to these young men through weekly devotionals, practices, and game time. Our head coach loves the Lord and is building a community of young men. He is trying to mold them into family and train them, not only to be better football players but also to be better husbands and fathers and men later in life. I have gotten to talk to these young men in the midst of adversity about biblical manhood and character on and off the field.*
> *— T. J. Tamer*

In this case the student pastor found an advocate in a believing coach. Another student pastor asked a local middle school how they could help:

> *We adopted the local middle school. We met with the principle and a team of teachers to discover how we can serve them and their students. What we discovered was about five things we could help with. We*

chaperone dances, provide food for teachers on important occasions, we are there for support and service on student recognition days, etc. We have titled our ministry to the middle school G.L.O.W (God's Love Our Work).
— *Chad Reister*

Back Up Before You Proceed

After the Green Bay Packers lost a football game they should have easily won, famous coach Vince Lombardi said to his team: "We are starting with the basics. This is a football."

You're a student pastor or a volunteer in your church's student ministry. You're reading this because you can't wait to get out. You love students and want to minister to them on their turf. "I like challenges. Bring it on!" you may be thinking.

Stop and ask yourself why there needs to be a student ministry in the first place. I know that sounds like we are taking three steps forward and two steps back, but if we don't understand why a student ministry needs to exist, then we have no reason to invite students into our local churches when we get out. The student ministry does exist to build up the students already in our respective churches so that they may become men and women of God, but that is not its sole purpose. The easiest thing to do as student pastors and leaders is to focus on the students we already have. God brought them to you and you never had to go anywhere. Wrong. Perhaps God showed favor on the children's ministry and perhaps the children's pastor worked very hard to cultivate a great environment for the children and their families. Now it's time for you to cultivate that same welcoming environment. What better way to welcome students than to go them?

> Your student ministry exists to make disciples who make disciples. You cannot do that by only meeting weekly in your church facility.

Let's perform a demographic study together. How many students are in your general area? You can do this by town, city, or region if you're in the middle of an area. For example, I could use Cary, North Carolina, but it might be more effective looking at all of West Raleigh as that is the general region in which people live. For the sake of the example, we will say that a given community has 1,200 students middle and high school aged. Now, think about how many students you have on average each week. Let's say your church is the largest in the area with about 100 students. Next, consider how many students are involved in all the Bible-believing churches in your area. Let's say the total is 250. That means about 350 students actively attend biblical churches in your community. It's easy to have the mindset that focuses on those you already have, especially if you are one of the largest ministries. It's easy to develop the mindset that you have "arrived" as a ministry, that you have plenty of students to whom you can minister. But look at the numbers above. If some 350 students actively attend in one area then that means 850 are not being reached. That is more than double the number already reached. Who cares for these students?

I'm not arguing that we need to choose between either caring for our current students or reaching those who we have not reached. We must do both, but the more we focus outwardly, the more we accomplish both--not so if we only focus on those we already reached. When you do get a chance to reach the unreached, remember what you're trying to do: promote your church. I'm just kidding, although that's what many believe.

When I go on campus or receive the opportunity to meet students who don't know Jesus, I have this mindset: I'm here to promote Jesus, not my church. That may sound counterintuitive, but if we promote ourselves before we exalt Christ then we have already started with the wrong motivation. There is already too much rivalry between ministries in a given area; let's make Jesus famous. When the gospel is preached, people will come. By all means, invite people to your church, but don't invite them for the sake of inflating the numbers. Invite them because you want to introduce them not only to Jesus, but also to His family, your community of faith. I believe that if we have the right motivation for getting out, that is to reach people with the gospel, great things will happen because God will be magnified!

Hindrances to Getting Out

I'm a University of North Carolina Tar Heels fan in every sport, not just basketball. I've been this way since I was nine years old, so you can judge if you want, but I won't change! In recent years their football program has greatly improved, but one thing consistently holds them back: themselves. It seems like every time I read the news someone has been accused of cheating in the classroom. Many times I've watched a game where the number of penalties on the team seem to directly affect their chances of winning. I would submit that student pastors have the same issue in a much greater matter. We forget to get out of our own way in order to let God do a great work in our respective ministries and us. I want to show you a few ways in which we get in our own way and how God can give us strength in each of these weaknesses.

The first challenge that we face is the institutionalization of the church. While the church does bring in money through tithes and offerings or some other sources, the church's primary goal is not to operate as a business. When we operate as a business, we begin to see people as property or assets with checkbooks that can help grow the church. People and their money do not grow a church. God grows His church. People invite others to church and want to see their church grow out of the love they have for God. In an institutional church, the lead pastor may often be seen as the CEO, the budget and finance committee as the CFO collectively, and all the other pastors and staff as numerous general managers. While there are management skills that must take place within a church, the primary goal of each staff member should be to make Jesus famous through the outpouring of their lives into the church for the glory of God. The path of least resistance in student ministry is to do everything in the institution rather than to advance a gospel movement.

Remember the Alamo? It started as a mission, became a battlefield, and is now a museum. That is also the story of institutional churches that lose a passion for gospel advance.

The second challenge to a potentially thriving student ministry and the goal of getting out is the laziness and comfort we feel in our job. I put these two things together because when we become comfortable, our comfort very quickly turns into laziness. Comfort comes from a myriad of factors. People could make you comfortable by consistently telling you how great a job you're doing, even though you don't feel that you've done much. Heed some of these comments, as they will lift you up when you're having a dark day in ministry, but don't listen to these comments alone. Your salary package may make you comfortable. Yes, I said it. If we're being real we must admit that money brings financial security and that can make us comfortable. When money makes you comfortable start giving it away. Make sure you're giving to your church as well as meeting other needs through your offerings. The last thing you and I need is a paycheck to actually keep us from working hard for the cause of Christ. It sounds ironic, but it can happen. Have people in your life who ask you what your daily goals, weekly goals, and long-term goals are. They will push you because they want to see you grow. When laziness subsides, getting out into the community begins.

One final challenge that student pastors face as they work to get out into the community to build up gospel-centered student ministries is fear. I'm both admitting my own shortcoming while calling out a shortcoming of others. I am doing so in love. When we already have a decent group and folks are content with us maintaining the status quo, why should we take the risk of meeting with principals and trying to minister on the school campus? And, sometimes we honestly are just more comfortable around churched students than lost youth in our community.

What do we have to fear? We have the sovereign God who has ordained us and called us to lead His people, namely students. We are to gather students with the goal to build up the church by the addition of students and their families. It's easy to worry about what a school official might say if we show up on their campus. As long as you follow the rules on campus, you have nothing to fear. In chapter three, some practical ways to get out will be given. For now, I want to help us all understand that fear is normal. In fact, if we don't have a healthy amount of fear in understanding the task at hand, then we fail to have proper reverence for the Lord, who called us to that task. If you're afraid of getting out, don't worry. Many start that way and most continue to get some butterflies. When we realize why we are doing what we are doing as well as who is going before us, it suddenly gets a bit easier.

I went on campus at a high school in Georgia. At the time, I was an intern at a church in the Atlanta area. I always thought that going on campus was something student pastors should be doing, i.e., a great idea, but I didn't know where to start. Finally, someone pushed me to go on campus. There I stood in the front office, a box of donuts in hand, smiling and waiting to talk to someone. The receptionist looked at me and asked what at the moment was a very hard question: "Can I help you?" I had no idea what to say. I introduced myself sheepishly and gave her the donuts, stating that they were for the office staff. She smiled, said thank you and immediately started helping the next person in line. I stood there looking around for fifteen minutes and left, a moment of awkwardness I will never forget.

When we get out into the community, these awkward moments will happen. But this is not the time to give up; it is the time to resolve to do whatever it takes to establish a ministry to the campus. Remain faithful and willing to dive into the lives of students surrounding your church. Hold on tight as we continue to understand how to get out effectively in order to advance the Kingdom of God through the lives of teenagers.

Food for Thought

- How does reaching out to the schools and your community fit into your church's mission statement?
- What are the main obstacles to getting out to your schools?
- What are ways you can currently try to serve your local school or build relationships with school officials?

CHAPTER 2

Get In the Community:
Relocate Your Ministry

> *"The worst mistake has been that Christians have tried to make their church programs or worship services their third place other than their home or workplace [or school] where they can relax and be in good company on a regular basis. The key is that third places need to be in public zones."*

> — Hugh Halter and Matt Smay,
> *The Tangible Kingdom*[6]

Think of the names of young people in your community. Picture their faces. Visualize their families, their hopes and dreams. Now, picture one specific youth you met at a school. Remember a conversation with a specific student with whom you have recently interacted.

Now consider this: how many students do you know well who are not involved in any church? Picture the young man who is into sports, but has no church background. Think about the young lady hungry for a relationship, but who has never really seen a healthy one as she comes from a home of deep brokenness. Can you see these faces? When you are involved in student ministry, it's easy to be so focused on the students you already have that you can forget about the many in your town who do not know Jesus, including some who would not even enter your church building. You will only reach them if you get out into the community. Like Jamie did.

Jamie met Renee, a 19-year-old who had been characterized by drug abuse, cutting, and pretty much anything other than church involvement. When he first met her he and his friends invited her into their lives, to pray for her and care for her. Jamie describes his encounter with Renee:

She has known such great pain; haunted dreams as a child, the near-constant presence of evil ever since. She has felt the touch of awful naked men, battled depression and addiction, and attempted suicide. Her arms remember razor blades, fifty scars that speak of self-inflicted wounds. Six hours after I meet her, she is feeling trapped, two groups of "friends" offering opposite ideas. Everyone is asleep. The sun is rising. She drinks long from a bottle of liquor, takes a razor blade from the table and locks herself in the bathroom.

Jamie said Renee cut her arm up with a razor and when she sought to enter a treatment center the next day, the nurse at the center called her too great a risk, refusing to accept her. "For the next five days," Jamie said, "She is ours to love. We become her hospital and the possibility of healing fills our living room with life. It is unspoken and there are only a few of us, but we will be her church, the body of Christ coming alive to meet her needs, to write love on her arms."

The movement that has spread globally to help young people trapped in issues of despair like cutting, eating disorders, and suicide was birthed from a young adult guy who with his friends cared for an older teenager that most would write off — like the nurse — as "too great a risk." Jamie's summary of what he learned from Renee, as he and his friends loved her and helped her before getting her to another treatment center.

Sunday night is church and many gather after the service to pray for Renee, this her last night before entering rehab. Some are strangers but all are friends tonight. The prayers move from broken to bold, all encouraging. We're talking to God but I think as much, we're talking to her, telling her she's loved, saying she does not go alone. One among us knows her best. Ryan sits in the corner strumming an acoustic guitar, singing songs she's inspired.

After church our house fills with friends, there for a few more moments before goodbye. Everyone has some gift for her, some note or hug or piece of encouragement. She pulls me aside and tells me she would like to give me something. I smile surprised, wondering what it could be. We walk through the crowded living room, to the garage and her stuff.

She hands me her last razor blade, tells me it is the one she used to cut her arm and her last lines of cocaine five nights before. She's had it with her ever since, shares that tonight will be the hardest night and she shouldn't have it. I hold it carefully, thank her and know instantly that this moment, this gift, will stay with me. It hits me to wonder if this great feeling is what

Christ knows when we surrender our broken hearts, when we trade death for life.

We often ask God to show up. We pray prayers of rescue. Perhaps God would ask us to be that rescue, to be His body, to move for things that matter. He is not invisible when we come alive. I have seen that this week and honestly, it has been simple: Take a broken girl, treat her like a famous princess, give her the best seats in the house . . . Tell her something true when all she's known are lies. Tell her God loves her. Tell her about forgiveness, the possibility of freedom, tell her she was made to dance in white dresses. All these things are true.

This story lies behind the global movement called To Write Love on Her Arms.[7] Jamie offers a dramatic example of what happens when we get out into the culture to care for people. Your local schools have more than a few young men and women with similar circumstances as Renee. You may not have a global impact, but you can help care for people Jesus died for who think no one cares about. But how can you get out?

Jesus Got Out

Read through the Gospels and you will find Jesus conducting most of His public ministry *publicly*, i.e. out among people. He earned terms of derision like "friends of sinners" by being among people outside the religious establishment of His day. That doesn't mean you need to become a bar hopper to be like Jesus. But it does mean you need to be out in the community if you will follow Him.

Of the 40 miracles recorded in the book of Acts, 39 happened outside a religious building.

In Matthew 9 we read of the love of Jesus and the urgency He had for those who were often rejected by the so-called spiritual people of His time. He went to every town, which means He was active in going from place to place. He preached the good news, He taught, and He touched––He healed people. But as He ministered, He stopped and observed the people around Him.

Jesus saw the multitude. How do you see people? Go to the local school and see the groups: jocks, nerds, preps, Goths, and so on. Is that how Jesus saw the crowd? No, He saw them as scattered––the best translation would be "harassed," as it comes from a term meaning "mangled by wild beasts."

Once, I (Alvin) was preaching at a rural church in eastern North Carolina. The pastor complained about the lack of youth in his small church. I asked him what the youth did, and he said they hung out at a place down by the river where they were obviously up to no good. After a couple of days at the meeting and no youth except the pastor's own children came, he again commented about the lack of youth. I asked him for an ice cooler. I took it in the truck I owned to a nearby store and filled it with ice and sodas. I picked the pastor up and said, "Let's go."

He asked me where we were going, and I told him to show me where the youth hung out. We pulled in and they looked at us with suspicion, two grown men in a truck at about 10 PM. I got out and smiled and began handing sodas to them. As they realized we were not there to criticize them, to tell them to go home, or to complain, but that we came to show love and to share Christ, they became remarkably responsive to us. Apparently, not many adults had been doing that.

> Try this: Go to a youth "hang out," a Third
> Place where they congregate, and serve
> them. Buy them lattes at Starbucks or milk
> shakes at McDonalds; provide sodas at the
> park. Identify their hangouts and serve
> them on their turf.

It's a lot easier to complain about the problems of youth than to go and become a part of their lives. But when we see people as Jesus sees them, we see not a variety of affinity groups, but as either lost or saved, and in need of the gospel.

When Jesus saw the crowd He was moved with compassion. The word means the intestines, or the gut. This kind of compassion is like a kick in the gut. I remember hearing about a woman in a major city who gave her 13 year old daughter to drug pushers to be their sex slave in order to feed her drug habit. If that does not hurt you deeply, you have lost the ability to hurt. All of us are moved with urgency to care about something. What do we care about most? If we keep before us the lostness of the world, and the need of young people without Christ in our communities, we will move to compassionate action. But if we are self-centered and just care about our own little youth group empire, we will not be so easily moved. Things that matter moved the people used by God in great spiritual awakenings.

One of the reasons we need to get out more is simply to be among the lost and outside our Christian subculture. Sitting in a local coffee shop and being aware of the conversations around us can help us to see people with fresh eyes. Spending time on the public school campus, learning from administrators, coaches and teachers the needs they face daily can help us as well. But nothing will help us to see people as Jesus sees them and be moved to action than studying the Scriptures and learning more and more about Jesus Himself. As we know Jesus more, we will see others more as He sees them. But we also must be among people to hear them, know them, and relate to them well.

How to Get Out

The first place to get out is the local public school. The public school is arguably the greatest mission field in America. When I (Josh) served at First Baptist Church, Woodstock, I was given Etowah High School as my primary mission field. Since I had played sports in high school, I quickly got to know several coaches while also working with students from church to get to know other students there. FCA meetings and ball games became great arenas for reaching out. Sure, some students on campus wondered why I was there, but over time they understood I simply wanted to serve them, their campus and their teachers.

I (Alvin) teach a course on missional student ministry at Southeastern Seminary with Jeff Lovingood, the Next Generation Pastor at Long Hollow Baptist Church near Nashville, Tennessee. A veteran of student ministry for decades, Jeff knows better than just about anyone how to get into schools. From serving on a coaching staff for the local football team to developing ministries in schools through teachers and administrators, Jeff helps student pastors to learn how to minister to schools. The key, Jeff observes, is to develop ministry in the school through the administration of the school rather than through the students, who come and go quickly. "Youth ministers like to work with students and try to reach the schools from the students up, but the way to reach the campus is to start with the administration."

If you are new in an area, think about these three ways of connecting with a local school.

First, look up. Before going to a school, spend time praying to God about that school. Ask Him for favor with the leaders there, for wisdom as you interact with them, and for an open door for the gospel. We need the work of the Spirit to do the work of the Kingdom!

Second, look in. That is, look inside your church to see who is already in the schools. Perhaps you have a teacher or administrator in your church. You certainly have students. Find out what God is already doing and whom He has placed there. That also means looking in other churches, talking to other student pastors to learn what they know about the schools. You also have people ready to serve. Jeff Lovingood tells about a time he went to a school and met the principal. He found out when they did their in-service training. He volunteered to feed all the teachers and staff. He had no budget to do this, but went to the people in the church, and laity came out of the woodwork to grill, chop, bake, and serve those folks. Now his church hosts five annual school graduations and has chaplains at several schools.

Finally, look out. Get out to the school, looking out for ways to see God at work already. Sitting down with a principal to find ways to serve the school is a great place to start.

Perhaps you are thinking something like this: Yes, I know we should be out in the community, and I know there are huge megachurches that have the money and people to impact a community. But my church is smaller, and we do not have the resources big churches have. We want to share with you stories from churches that are not massive. For instance, Mike Camire is a graduate of Southeastern Seminary and was in the first student ministry class I (Alvin) taught a few years back. Mike has been student pastor at Parkway Baptist Church, a young church planted about a decade ago near Richmond, Virginia. Parkway is a growing, healthy church, but a long way from being a megachurch. Here are some things Mike has developed as he leads there:[8]

> *One part of our ministry that we have been doing for four years now is our "Tailgate Crew" ministry. We provide a free tailgate for students before football games at several schools in our area. We show up about two hours before kick-off, find a prime location in the parking lot at the school, set up our equipment, and start cooking hot dogs! I have a group of adults from our church that are a part of our weekly small groups that help me each time we do a tailgate. They have made it their group's mission project. They pretty much run everything for me, which allows me to mix it up with students! Each summer I contact the athletic directors at the schools that we want to tailgate at and let*

them know what I want to do and make sure it is okay with them. Most of the time I get an overwhelmingly positive response from each director I contact.

The reason we do this is to provide a free and safe environment for students to gather and have a good time before a football game. Several years ago our county was having problems with students leaving school, going to a student's house, getting drunk, and then showing up to the game. By providing a free tailgate, it gives students something fun and exciting to come to before the game! It also gives our students an opportunity to invite their friends to something fun that their church does! It is much easier for students to get friends to come to a tailgate at their school than to a Sunday service. Our students are given special "Tailgate Crew" t-shirts that they wear on game-day as a way to invite and promote the tailgate. The students then connect with those that they have invited at the tailgate and it allows me and other adult leaders to meet and connect with their friends.

We will have anywhere from 250 to 300 folks come through our tailgates each time we do them. We have been asked by one high school in our area the last two years to provide a tailgate as part of their homecoming festivities in which we saw almost 700 people come through the tailgate each time! We have also been asked by a middle school in our area the last two years to provide a tailgate for folks coming to their faculty vs. student charity basketball game. This ministry has been an incredible element in our ministry that pushes students out of their comfort zones to invite people to the tailgate and connect with them when they show up. It also challenges our adults that help out by connecting and building relationships with those that come by the tailgate.

Mike adds a few features they use in these tailgates:

1. *Upbeat music bumping through a NICE sound system - I play anything from Lecrae and his 116 Clique, Thousand Foot Krutch, Club/DJ type music, to even some secular music. It is a very eclectic mix which is able to connect with folks who like all different genres*

2. *Corn hole and ladder-ball games*

3. *Free hot dogs, chips, canned drinks/ bottle water (hot chocolate when it is cold), popcorn, and sweet treats!*

In addition to the tailgates at the fall football games, Mike and his church are involved in the community in others ways, like purchasing yearbook ads for sports programs at the public schools. A few other ideas they use:

- They provide lunches for teachers and leaders at several schools during the year;
- They mentor at risk teenaged boys at a local middle school. Here is how:

The school asked us to provide some mentors for a group of 6th graders who were at risk. Our mentors go in and teach a lesson each week (on whatever they choose) and spend time living life on life with the boys. The goal is for the mentors to stay together with the same group of boys until they move on to high school. Last year this group was able to take a "field trip" to our church and have an end of the year cookout!

Mike and his ministry also take advantage of an opportunity in the school schedule:

Every other month here, our students have an early release day where they get out of school three hours early. I took advantage of this and started having what I called "Early Release Day Celebration Lunches" at a local CiCi's Pizza. At these lunches, I connect with our students and encourage them to bring their friends so I can meet them and build relationships with them. To encourage students to bring friends, I offered to pay for their friends' meals. It has been awesome to see what God has done with this! We started out with about 20 students and have had as many as 70! I have had a lot of great conversations with students that probably would never step inside of a church!

Try this: look at regular activities in your local school calendar to see whether you might partner with them, like the Release Day mentioned by Mike Camire.

Mike not only looks for ways he and other adults in his church can get out, but he also pushes his students to do so as well, helping them to live missionally:

When it comes to being missional, our students are always encouraged to live each day of their life as if they were on a mission trip . . . because they are! It is and has always been part of our church's DNA to be a missional people both here and abroad. In everything we do, we strive to make it missional. Here are some more specific ways that our students are being missional:

1. *Because we have been casting and speaking missional vision to our students, a group of high schoolers decided to take it a step further and create a Christian club at their school called TGIF (Thank God It's Friday). All of the student leadership in this club are from Parkway. They get together every Thursday night to plan the next day's meeting. They meet at 6:45 a.m. in a classroom at the school, lead worship, and a Bible study for students that want to come. They have a consistent group of about 30 students who come and who are from all different faith backgrounds. Recently I was at the school and a teacher came up to me and shared with me how impressed she was at the leadership and maturity of the students who lead TGIF. These are some of my top core students and I am very proud that they have stepped out in faith to lead this club at their school!*

2. *We give out prayer cards each Sunday morning that include four prayer points that we pray for together each Sunday morning and that the students take with them and pray over each day of the week. The points include (1) an*

unreached people group; (2) a North American Mission Board "Send City"--a city targeted by our denomination (the Southern Baptist Convention) for ministry and church planting; (3) a missionary partner that our church is partnered with; and (4) a church planter from our state. By doing this, we keep this info in front of our students and pray that God would call them out to join God in his mission in reaching an unreached people group, serve in a NAMB Send City, go and work with one of our missionary partners, and be a church planter or church planters wife.

3. Summer camp and mission trips are a huge part of a student ministry. The camp that has worked for us and our missional vision is LifeWay's Mission-Fuge (M-Fuge). We have been going to M-Fuge for 11 years and God has done some amazing things through the ministry of this camp. M-Fuge is a summer camp with a missional twist. Each day of the camp, participants spend close to 4-5 hours out in a community where the camp is located doing mission work. Our students love it more and more each year we go! We started

going to M-Fuge with 30 people and now take about 150. This is a great way to get our students involved in a basic missions experience. From there, our students are encouraged to go with us on an overseas missions experience through IMB's International World Changers. IWC gives our students a great opportunity to experience God in a global context. We have seen God do some amazing things through these different experiences and call students to serve all over the world as a result!

4. *In sticking with the missional vision of our student ministry, our Disciple-Now weekend that we do each and every year is missional. We call it LIVE LOVE and it is a weekend that we take our students around our community and set-up opportunities for them to serve others.*

5. *Each Fall, around See You at the Pole, we have our students participate in a Life Book saturation. The Life Book is a ministry of the Gideons. They encourage student ministries to challenge and train their students to hand out these Life Books in their schools. The Life Book*

gives a simple tool to students to help them get God's Word and the gospel into the hands of others at their school. Over the last two years our students have given out over 2000 Life Books. We have seen some of our most shy students take several of these Life Books and give them out and share their faith! It is a great tool for students to use to share the gospel with students at their schools.

We wanted you to hear from real life student pastors who are getting out and making an impact in their communities. Mike's example is one you can learn from and follow.

Food for Thought

- What are ways you are getting out right now that you have found to be effective?
- What are ways you can be more involved in the local schools and the community?
- How can you help get your students and adult leaders involved?
- Are there specific ways you can begin to get out more (like doing office work at a Starbucks rather than at the church building, or connecting more with a school sports team)?

- Who are leaders (adult and student) who are already living this way or who want to be more engaged in the community? How can you partner with them to get out?

CHAPTER 3

GET BUSY:
Practical Ways to Get Out

"We often miss opportunity because it's dressed in overalls and looks like work."
--Thomas Edison

"The main thing is not to be a stranger to the school. Don't be some strange preacher guy; build relationships over time with the administration." — Student Pastor John Walker

---

I (Josh) walked into the locker room. I knew no one. Feeling very sheepish, I found one of the guys standing there and asked where the head coach was. Football season had just begun and a local high school invited me to give a devotion or motivational speech. To say I was giddy would be an understatement. I had been praying that I would have an avenue to be on campus. I met the head coach of the team and he told me to wait for a few minutes so he could get the guys together. I said hello to some guys, not knowing any of them. Once the time to speak came, I was tongue-twisted, nervous and concerned that if I said the wrong thing I may turn into the next tackling dummy at the following practice. Scared. Awkward. Unsure of myself. Have you ever felt these emotions when talking to students? Do you currently feel these emotions about the idea of getting out to do the work of the ministry? Clearly I did and on certain days I still do. When we finally decide to get out, we pray for boldness.

For you grammar gurus, I put that last statement in the present tense on purpose. Praying for boldness is not something we only do when we get out of the office. We need to constantly pray for boldness in every aspect of our lives (Acts 4:29-31). Pray for boldness when you prepare a message, when you prepare a small group lesson, or when you go to lunch with a student in order to disciple him or her. I believe God will give us boldness if we ask for it (2 Cor. 3:12). I imagine it would be helpful to have some practical ways to get out. I'm sure that will increase your boldness! In this chapter, we will look at how Jesus got out and how the Holy Spirit is with you wherever you may go in each situation. My prayer is that God will speak to you and give you confidence to get out even today in order to reach others with the gospel message.

Lessons from Jesus

I don't know much, but what I do know is that before we see some practical ways to get out from fellow student pastors, and me, we must first look to Jesus and the example He set. In Matthew 9, Christ called Matthew to be His disciple. Matthew was at his "office," which was a tax booth. We know he was a tax collector and we know most hated him because of that fact. Jesus literally met him where he was and uttered two words: "Follow me" (Matt. 9:9). I wish I had that kind of power sometimes. Christ has great power and it is on display in this book. The Bible says that Matthew immediately arose and followed Jesus. What was the next thing they did? They ate! If you're a Southern Baptist, you're not surprised at all by this. It seems that if there's one thing we have perfected, it's eating lunch with other people. But notice the crowd surrounding Jesus. The text says, "Many tax collectors and sinners came and reclined with Jesus" (Matt. 9:10). Jesus ate with people who were not like Him! It doesn't say that Jesus is sinning with them or talking the way that they talk, but He entered their world. Be willing to enter into the world of your students, going where they go and experiencing, with wisdom in mind, what they experience.

Jesus knew his context. Do you know yours? What is your church known for in your community? Before you decide how you're going to get out effectively, you need to know your context. For example, if your church is known for having provided the team dinner for a local high school football team, you should continue to do that. Your starting point has been given to you. Thank the Lord and get after it! If you do have this opportunity, don't reinvent the wheel. In view of knowing your context, it might not be the best idea to do something else during the same season. They expect something to happen and it's your opportunity to provide that for them.

The 411 on Ministering in the Public School:

1. *It is intimidating. When you first go to a school, you will be nervous. It's ok. Meet the receptionist and the principal.*

2. *Ask the principal for permission to eat lunch with your students and as you do, ask, what are the rules?*

3. *In most states you can only sit down with your students from your church. Your students may act differently at school. The first week is hard. But once you get through it, it gets better. The most awkward time is when you have first and third lunch and sit there awkwardly in the middle time!*

4. *Follow the dress code. I never wear shorts or tee shirts. If I get to play ball with the students I never dress in the same room with the students. On those occasions I dress up and then change in the gym.*

— *Brian Mills*

Another aspect related to knowing your context involves not pushing the envelope or doing too much too soon. I'm sure someone is reading this who simply wants some practical ways to get out. Let me calm you down a bit. Our calling is to be a shepherd to students rather than a drill sergeant. A shepherd loves his sheep more than his cause. A drill sergeant loves his cause more than his sheep. While the cause of reaching more people for the gospel is wonderful and necessary, we only minister well when we love the sheep, the students with whom we come in contact. The same goes for those in authority over them in schools. Jesus met sinners where they were. Jesus holds all authority to have the people do whatever He wanted them to do, yet His decision was to simply spend time with them, loving them first in order to lead them well.

Holding the mindset of a shepherd, remember that when you get out, it's okay to be one step ahead. For example, rather than asking a teacher if you can help them in any way, have a small list in your mind of ways you could offer to serve prior to meeting that teacher. This shows a couple of things. First, it shows that you mean what you say. Many people say they want to serve, but are not willing to seek out ways to serve. Second, it shows initiative. You're not backing them into a corner by making them decide how you can serve. Take note of needs around you and meet them. While it's okay to be one step ahead, it's not a wise idea to always be ten steps ahead. If you're one step ahead, you're a leader, but if you're ten steps ahead, you're an idiot. That may be harsh, but if we're going to minister well, we need to be willing to go one step at a time rather than making people drink out of a fire hydrant. Don't be that guy who goes into a school and immediately assumes you own the place. You don't. God does. He will do a good work in you. Take that passion and infuse it with great faithfulness. Remember that you can be so driven to reach people or do something new that you leave behind those you were called to serve.

> If you're one step ahead, you're a leader, but if you're ten steps ahead, you're an idiot.

In order to garner boldness to get out and do great ministry outside of the church office, we will first look at ways Jesus did ministry. They will remind us of the proper attitude to have when we get out.

The first way to get busy? *Love how Jesus loves.* This sounds cliché, but usually something becomes cliché because it's often very true. I think of two examples immediately. Luke 19 tells the story of Jesus going to the house of Zacchaeus, the house of the most hated individual in the community. As noted above, Matthew 9 tells of Jesus dining with Matthew, another tax collector whom everyone also hated. In each case, Jesus sought people out. He did not wait for these tax collectors to come to Him. Let's be real. They probably wouldn't come to Him because they knew how people within their occupation treated others and probably how He viewed that. Jesus met tax collectors, adulterers, the sick and needy with unfiltered love. Unfiltered because he did not love them based on their social or spiritual status. He did not filter it through an arbitrary process. Jesus loved them in spite of their gross and detestable ways. If you and I are going to get out and be like Jesus among students, we must be willing to love students and their families despite their shortcomings.

Give as Jesus gives. You may have figured this out by now, but getting out requires us to do something. In fact, that something may be the most uncomfortable thing you have ever done in ministry. Perhaps you're the student pastor who sits in your office from 9 AM to 5 PM with the exception of going out to lunch, and even then you go alone often. Jesus gave His life so that all may have eternal life. He continuously gives you and I grace. Consider that Christ allowed imperfect people to proclaim His perfect gospel in a full-time ministry setting. That's incredible grace! If Jesus gave His life, then we can give our time. Getting out will often require going somewhere early or going to a football game (yes, a football game) late in order to show love and support to the students you are trying to reach.

> When you get to your office on Monday, map out your week with coffee with a few students in mind, or with the local high school football team in mind.

You may see this final point coming. If we are going to get out into our community of students and their families we must not only love as Jesus loves or give as Jesus gives, but we must also *serve as Jesus serves*. In the Bible, Jesus served by washing His disciples' feet, sharing meals with others, and healing people of their sickness. If the Son of God could lower himself to foot-washing, then you and I can take some time to visit with the student who talks way too much, but may be seeking attention because he or she does not get the time of day at home. May the teachings of Jesus be what spur us on to being in the lives of our students. Let us not do it for selfish gain, but for the gain of the Kingdom.

Practical First Steps

I want to give a few very practical ways to be healthily busy with the opportunity of building up God's Kingdom in student ministry. These ways are not gospel, but I believe they are effective. Following this, I will offer advice given from fellow student pastors who know more than me. Remember: a smart man knows what he doesn't know.

First, go through the first door that opens on campus. I know that sounds churchy, but when a door is opened, I believe it is because God has opened it. More often than not, once you have met administrators, the Fellowship of Christian Athletes (FCA), Young Life, or something similar may be the widest door. These para-church organizations welcome student pastors with open arms. They are always looking for speakers and prayer partners to join them. True, we want to reach students who don't know the Lord with the gospel message and the best way to do that may be through the already established clubs on campus. Use these to your advantage, as representatives in that class also happen to be students and teachers on campus every day. You and I only get to spend a few hours a week on campus and even then we are old and out of touch to many of the students we encounter.

Second, practice the funnel principle wherever you are on campus. Matt Lawson, formerly the student pastor at First Baptist Church of Woodstock, Georgia and currently planting and pastoring Story City Church in Los Angeles, California, taught me this principle and I want to pass it on to others. A funnel is wide at the top and narrow at the bottom. When we enter a school, the first person we meet is the receptionist, or the widest part of the funnel. She holds the keys to the school. *The receptionist is key!*

We sign in with her, we tell her who we are there to see and why, and we see her when we sign out later. Essentially, if you don't have a good relationship with her, you probably won't have a great relationship with the rest of the school. Veteran student pastor Michael Wood is so right when he says the two most important people in the school are the principal and the receptionist.

Be honest and follow the rules when you meet the receptionist. She will greatly appreciate it and if all else fails, you can at least be a blessing to her. The second layer of the funnel principle is the principal, teachers, and coaches. This also includes the band director. They love their students and players. If you serve them, you will gain an opportunity to meet students. Meet the coaches and teachers who are involved in FCA. Offer services to the coaches throughout their many weeks of practices i.e. shagging foul balls that go over the fence in baseball practice or offering to help tutor students in different subjects. Bring Chick-fil-A to coaches doing film work for the next game. Performing a background check for the school will open many doors in this area.

The last practical item I want to give you also serves as the final part of the funnel principle. *Take students with you when you spend time with others!* The smallest part of the funnel is the students. If you've established great relationships with these other entities then students will start to wonder who you are and why you're there. The best way to have influence on the local students is to utilize students already in your local church. When I was an intern (and not filling up a water cooler with ice, etc.), I frequently would tell students in my local church what games I would attend and what days I would be serving on campus. This didn't happen every day, but when it did I had much more influence than when I went alone. I recall one day when I took freeze pops to the volleyball teams asking Aaron, a senior at the high school at the time, to come with me. Sure enough, there was great rapport because several of the players knew who he was.

They couldn't care any less about me and that's fine! A great work was being accomplished and it sparked a great relationship between myself and the volleyball coaches and players. Today, as a student pastor, I tell students when I'll be at their campus to accomplish the work of the ministry and the building up of God's Kingdom. It is truly amazing when students get excited about sharing their faith because they're seeing you attempt to do so. If you're not willing to get out and get busy sharing the gospel, don't be surprised if your students aren't either.

Many student pastors who get out have found the effectiveness (and its low budget!) of freeze pops for ball teams and marching bands.

Student Pastor Testimonies

For the duration of this chapter, I want to get out of the way and allow you to hear from fellow student pastors. Some are current and some are former student pastors, but all have much to say on the subject. Concerning how to get into the lives of students, the first thoughts come from Matthew Sawyer. Before you see this, I want you to understand his heart for getting out in order to get into the community. He admits, "I am always looking for ways to get uncomfortable and outside the walls of the church campus." For many of us, getting out is difficult simply because of discomfort. Jesus said blessed are the humble, not blessed are the comfortable. Here is some of what Matt has been able to do by the grace of God:

> *I have been connecting on campus when I can. We recently fed a marching band at a local high school. It was a great opportunity to invest into kids many churches may not connect with.*
>
> *It is nothing major but we will continue to do more of this. We also have a rescue mission that houses families in need of a place to stay in our community. We have gone to help serve on a Wednesday night and will also do a service in January. I desire for students to get outside of the church walls and engage the community and their peers at school. I encourage them to take leadership roles in their campus clubs at school. I have two middle school girls who coordinate their First Priority meetings. It is so great seeing them lead and they enjoy doing it!*[9]

You may see an admission that campus ministry is not easy, but it is both effective and worth the work and discomfort. They get out by going on campus and to a rescue mission. Getting out doesn't simply mean go on campus and do nothing else. Here we see that the whole church has bought into the idea of getting out. When your students see growth as a result of being out and about doing the work of Christ, I believe the rest of the church will follow. The next example is from Jason Engle,[10] pastor of students and discipleship at Westwood Baptist Church. It's a phenomenal example of the whole church getting on board with the "get out" mentality.

> *Last year I had the honor of being asked to serve as team chaplain for Person High School's varsity football team. During that season, I began to wonder how perhaps God could open doors to deeper ministry within the school through that opportunity. I recalled something that I had learned in Southeastern Seminary professor Bruce Ashford's Theology and Culture class. Good contextualization occurs on three levels: faithful, meaningful, and dialogical. I realized that by looking for more opportunities, I had become too narrowly focused on what I would want out of this opportunity, or how it could serve my own ends (which were gospel-focused, by the way). I realized that I needed to look for opportunities that would be*

meaningful to them and that I needed to seek to be more dialogical in my approach. With this in mind, I began to intentionally look for ways that our church or I could serve the members of this team that would be meaningful to them and to the community.

Part of this opportunity afforded me the wonderful opportunity to speak to the team at their Friday pre-game meals. The coach professed to be a believer, and offered me free reign as to what I could share!

At that time the team had these meals at our local Golden Corral restaurant. I began to wonder what the cost for these meals must be, and what the financial means were for providing them. I approached the coach with this question and discovered that individual coaches and players were responsible for the cost of these meals with some help from fundraising efforts by the boosters at football games. Usually the players/coaches were left to have to pay a good sum of money for the meals. As he explained that, I could tell that this proved burdensome to him and the team. Some players' families struggled to provide the money, and really he would love to see the funds raised at games go toward other needs.

Immediately I identified this as a need that could potentially be covered by our church that would prove incredibly meaningful to the players/coaches on the team, as well as the school and community. After conversations with my pastor and our elders, it was decided that we would ask the school if they would allow us to not only cover the cost of the team meals, but even host the team for these meals and prepare the food, all in our church building. The new coach at Person received an overwhelming 'yes' from the athletic director and we began to pray about making that happen.

The greatest hurdle in providing this type of service to the team, of course, centered upon the financial aspect. How will we pay to provide 11+ meals for 50-60 people during the course of the week? We arrived at a rather large amount of money that we determined it would take to make this happen, and we began to pray and discuss how the need would be met. Our church, like so many others, has struggled over the past couple of years to meet the demands of an already stripped down budget. The initial idea, as is usually the case, included a love offering to see how much of the needed amount could be raised.

My desire for our church, though, went much deeper than asking them to provide needed funds to provide meals. I wanted to find ways to enable as many people as possible to be a part of loving on these players and coaches and serving our community through this ministry. At a business meeting, of all places, where we were introducing this idea to our members, God reminded me of an old cliché, "many hands make light work." I began to do the math involved with this thought. Instead of attempting to come up with the large amount we had decided it would take to pull this off, what if we involved many people to come up with smaller amounts? The math determined that if we were to get 50+ sponsors (families or individuals), it would cost them $50 to sponsor one player/ coach for the entire season! Further, if we can find individual sponsors for each individual, this would open up a wonderful door of ministry apart from simply providing the financial means for the meals. So we asked families/ individuals in our church to sign up to sponsor an individual, and in doing so they would be committing to invest in them in the following three ways:

1. *Financially: Providing the necessary funds to feed them throughout the season at the pre-game meals.*

2. *Spiritually: Each sponsor is asked to write your player/coach a note of encouragement for the player to pick up at the pre-game meal and have prior to each week's game. Sponsors are asked to build relationships with their players through this forum...get to know them, invite them to come and sit with you at church one Sunday, look for opportunities to encourage or share the gospel, etc.*

3. *Prayerfully: Each sponsor will commit to pray for their specific player/coach each Friday at 4pm as I have the opportunity to speak the Word into their lives.*

My church blew me away with its response. We had every single player and coach sponsored in week one of asking for his or her help. I created a big board of envelopes. Each one had printed on it an individual's name, picture and number. Each sponsor also picked up a copy of what was printed on their individual's envelope with a magnet attached to take home and place on their fridge as a prayer reminded throughout the season. One of the incredible aspects of this ministry included the members of the church going above and beyond what had been asked. Members made posters for their player and hung them on the wall in the room where the meals took place. Members not only wrote encouragement cards, but also began to bring goodie bags for their player/coach, books for them to read, and gift cards from local fast food restaurants! Fridays became my favorite day of the week during the season, not only because of the time I got to spend with the team, but to see their faces light up as they walked through the door of our church and made a b-line toward the player board and goodie bag table!

Through those envelopes so many conversations began, with players dropping notes back into their envelope each week to be read by their sponsor. I cannot recall all the times the coaches and players have personally thanked both our church and me for treating them with such kindness. I continue to hear of a buzz in the community about our church and its heart for the football team and local high school. God has richly blessed this interaction with Person High School in this way just a couple of months after it was decided by the school board to remove any and all prayer from the school's most recent graduation.

What an incredibly powerful story of Jason getting out, willing to meet a need that was higher than what they alone could accomplish as a student ministry. God gave them great favor as an entire church family. They came together to meet the need, together to spread God's glorious gospel, and together for the building of the Kingdom of God. This is one of the best of examples of God's faithfulness to the Kingdom-minded desires of a local body.

I pray that you were able to receive some great, albeit extensive, practical advice in order to get out. When we get out, we must know that there is much to be done. We cannot do this alone. God is on our side and He has given us great resources and brothers and sisters in Christ to aid the mission. God calls us to a life on mission. As student pastors, we have one of the greatest and most fun opportunities. We work with people younger than us in almost every capacity. Be willing to do the work of Jesus. Be willing to love the people Jesus places in your life, saint and sinner alike. Be willing to take healthy risks in order to make the name of Jesus great. Be willing to garner boldness and get busy sharing the gospel outside of the comfortable confines of your church office.

Food for Thought

- Do you know the principal at the primary middle and high schools to whom you minister?

More importantly, do they know you? What can you do to get to know them better?

- What examples from student pastors you've read so far could be implemented by your ministry?
- Would it help to take this book and get with a few fellow student pastors in your area and pray together, followed by a discussion of how you might serve together to impact your schools?

CHAPTER 4

GET PERSONAL:
Love God, Love People

> "One of the great uses of Twitter and Facebook will be to prove at the Last Day that prayerlessness was not from lack of time."— John Piper

Students love social media, and so do we. Social media can be used for great good to connect us, to help in the sharing of edifying information, and as an aid to mentoring. But anything with the potential for good has the potential for harm, and social media has also brought great damage to many. Bullying online has become the third most cited reason for teen suicide, for instance. We may quote the old saying that "sticks and stones may break my bones, but words will never hurt me," but the saying isn't actually true. It can also be a remarkable time waster that interferes with real ministry.

What if we used our words to infuse life and joy and hope, whether on the Internet or in personal conversations? What if we helped students to recover the idea that the gospel means good news, and this news not only affects us spiritually, but also guides all our lives? What if we helped our students to live life focused on this simple phrase: "Love God, Love People." What if our words reflected that?

The young lady in your local school who just lost her virginity to her boyfriend—the same guy who now has no interest in her—does not care how cool your youth praise band is. The young man whose dad beats him and verbally abuses him every week has no interest in your latest T-shirt idea. And the parents down the street from your church that just discovered their son is an addict has no interest in your youth room's hip lighting. But they could all use someone to invest in them and to show and share the light and hope of Jesus.

Indicative and Imperative

If we plan to get out into the community both personally and through those we lead, we must be clear on what it is that compels us to go in the first place. This involves both the *indicative* of the gospel and the *imperative* of the gospel. The indicative refers to the beautiful gospel in all its glory, the greatest news we could ever know, and what being changed by the good news means: forgiven, covered by His grace, and in fellowship with God, which infuses us with a love for God and others. The more we help students to understand who they are in Christ, the more likely they will see it as good news and want to share it with others. The imperative refers to what we do now that we are changed and being increasingly conformed to the image of Christ: we live to worship Him and to fulfill the Great Commission He gave us. Being able to have conversations centered on the gospel lies at the very center of our getting out, after all.

Seeing the Gospel in Its Greatness

In his history of youth ministry *When God Shows Up*, Mark Senter argues that recent student ministry has tended--like all of the church I would argue--to swing back and forth "between stressing the gospel in a narrow sense and exploring the gospel in a more holistic manner." He continues:

> *In its narrow sense the Christian gospel stressed the good news of redemption through Jesus Christ; in its broader sense the Christian gospel emphasized the entire story of redemptive history that embraced the kingdom of God. In its narrow sense the Christian gospel in youth ministry transformed young people; in its broader sense the Christian gospel transformed youth culture. In its narrow sense the Christian gospel in youth ministry stressed salvation; in its broader sense the Christian gospel focused on the changes in the lives of young people in whom salvation was applied.*[11]

Today for a variety of reasons the church in general and student ministry in particular must focus on the more broad sense of the gospel. I (Alvin) articulate this more in *As You* Go, but in summary my reasons for arguing for a whole-Bible approach to the gospel is due to the fact that Western culture no longer has the biblical mindset it once had, that the church has lost the "home field" advantage, and that examples in the Scripture (like Paul in Acts 17 at Mars Hill) of gospel proclamation to people outside the Judeo-Christian worldview requires a more wide-screen look at the gospel from Creation to the Cross. Missionaries in unreached lands have long argued for an approach of storying the gospel in terms of its grand narrative.

For the past several years I have shared the gospel to unbelieving and believing youth from the perspective of the metanarrative of the Scripture: Creation, Fall, Rescue, and Restoration. I use the Story (see viewthestory.com) and have taught this to many student pastors who have in turn used this in their ministries. More recently I have employed the 3 Circles approach to sharing Christ developed by my friend Jimmy Scroggins, pastor of the First Baptist Church of West Palm Beach, Florida, and used by the North American Mission Board of the Southern Baptist Convention. As you will see, both of these have many similarities in their approach.

As Josh started his ministry at his current church, he walked students through the Story as well, because he wanted his students both to understand the wonderful Story of the gospel and have an effective way of sharing it.

Four "P's" For Sharing the Gospel

But before we jump into a way of sharing Christ, here are some things to remember as you help students learn to share Christ. I call it the Four P's that serve to encourage us in our task:

1) Prayer. Sharing Christ does not compare to a sales pitch. We share what God has done, the announcement of good news, not a bit of advice to help folks. It's supernatural work. The early church knew that. In fact, the early church was birthed out of a prayer meeting. Notice: In Acts 1:14, the early believers prayed in unison for the ten days from the ascension of Jesus to the day of Pentecost as Jesus has told them. In 2:42 even as the church was born they devoted themselves to the apostles' teaching and to prayers.

In Chapter 3 they were going to pray when they met a lame man. He was healed and began to praise God (wouldn't you?), and he joined Peter and John as they entered the temple to pray. In fact, as you read through the story of gospel advance in the Acts, you will see that prayer laid the foundation of everything they did.

Take a minute to read Acts 4:23-31. In this passage they faced their first persecution, and we read their prayer. They did not ask God to make it easier in the face of persecution, they did this: 1) They "prayed" the gospel (23-28); they started with a sovereign God, then affirmed Him as Creator, then recognized the fallenness of man ("the heathen rage," etc.). Then they acknowledged Jesus' work for salvation was God's plan all along. 2) They asked God to give them boldness to proclaim the gospel. 3) God answered! The place shook, they were all filled with the Spirit, and they all continued to share Christ with boldness.

Whatever you do to get out into the community and to get your students out sharing Christ, build your efforts on much prayer. I recently led a huge team of Southeastern students to do outreach in Baltimore for a week. One team leader came to me after the first couple of days frustrated at the reception they received. We talked, and he led his team to fast and pray, seeking the Lord's favor. The next day they led nine to Jesus. Prayer matters.

Try this 3-fold prayer I pray and challenge my students to pray: God give me 1) An opportunity to witness today 2) wisdom to see it 3) boldness to seize it.

---

2) *Power.* In Acts 1:8, Jesus called His followers to be witnesses. Our goal in witnessing is not to show how theologically brilliant or how clever we are, but to partner with the Holy Spirit. He convicts people of sin (John 16), and He brings people from death to life.

Witnessing is less a *presentation* we dump on people and more a *conversation* we have with people. The more we know Jesus, the more we understand the wonder of the gospel, and the more we know how the Spirit works, the more we can converse with others about Jesus.

The Spirit *fills* the believer for service. He gives us *boldness* to witness. He provides divine appointments as we obey.

The Spirit *convicts* unbelievers of sin (John 16). He *leads* them to witnesses (Cornelius in Acts 10, the Eunuch in Acts 8, etc.). He brings a lost person from death to life.

Few things will excite your students and help them to grow in Christ more than seeing the Spirit lead them in their daily lives. The Spirit teaches us through the Word, and He guides us to opportunities to witness.

3) *Proclamation* (Matthew 28:16-20). This is where we actually proclaim the good news (I explain in more detail how to do this below). Living witnesses sharing Christ are God's Plan A, and He has not given us a Plan B!

4) *Persuasion* (II Corinthians 5:9-21). When we do share Christ, we need to ask people to respond to the gospel.

Our culture is so driven by political correctness we don't even see how timid we have become. But the gospel in its very essence requires a response. Paul said, knowing the fear of the Lord, being aware that although we are loved by Him and secure in Him, we obey Him in being ministers of reconciliation.

If you are a believer and are breathing, I like to say, you are a missionary. In this lesson I would explain how to lead someone to Christ and how to do initial follow-up and explain some tips on maintaining a relationship when they say no. As you help students share Christ, and as you share Christ, give attention to calling people to follow Christ when we witness. Using a gospel booklet, especially when initially learning to share Christ, will help a witness to do that.

Try this: Get one (or both) of these two great gospel booklets: *The Story* by spreadtruth.com, and the *Life on Mission 3 Circles* booklet by the North American Mission Board namb.net. Give copies to your students and ask them to give to friends with this introduction: "This booklet is a short Bible study explaining the what the Bible is all about."

How to Share the Gospel

This week, pay attention to conversations you have with people. Notice how often people talk about their PAIN or their PASSION, i.e., they talk about something that is not right (something little like a flat tire or long hours at work, or something major like cancer or a breakup; or, they talk about their hopes, dreams, or something good that just happened). Begin to ask the Spirit to give you ears to hear so you can apply the gospel to their pain or passion.

I love helping youth have conversations with friends about Christ, not by dumping the gospel on them like an ice bucket challenge, but by starting with a normal conversation about non-spiritual things (at least on the surface), and moving the conversation to the work of Jesus for our salvation. One way I do this is from the perspective of movies. The movies we know and love follow well-known plotlines. I just watched *Guardians of the Galaxy* from Marvel Comics. Like most adventure movies, it follows the plotline "man falls in hole and is rescued." Everything from *Rambo* to *Die Hard*, from *The Expendables* to *The Avengers* follows this storyline. So does every episode of the *Power Rangers*, which Josh and many of his age watched as children.

A version of this plotline is "kill the dragon, get the girl" in which not only is someone rescued out of some real or out of a metaphorical pit, but a damsel in distress is saved from some evil person or beast. *Taken* serves as a recent example, not to mention a lot of cheesy movies from the Sci-Fi network.

Then we have another whole genre, the romantic comedy, or "boy meets girl." From *The Proposal* to *Hitched*, this storyline features a boy meeting a girl or vice versa, after which we learn a couple of things: guys are dumb (just watch the movies to see how dumb), and girls are crazy (they overreact, etc.). But in the end, they finally connect and live happily ever after. We love these, don't we?

A final example, "rags to riches," follows the story of Cinderella or more recently *The Princess Diaries*. In all these storylines we see a similar pattern: a generally happy beginning, followed by tragedy, evil, someone or something evil (or a combination of these), followed by a rescue, a resolution, or some sort of dramatic change, ending in "they all lived happily ever after." We do love these, don't we?

The question is, why? Matt Chandler, Josh Patterson, and Eric Geiger help us to see this through the eyes of two literary greats, C.S. Lewis and J.R.R. Tolkien:

A conversation once held between colleagues C. S. Lewis and J. R. R. Tolkien speaks to this innate human desire for being part of larger-than-life stories, quests, and victories— the draw of our hearts toward "myths," which Lewis said were "lies and therefore worthless, even though breathed through silver." "No," Tolkien replied, "They are not lies." Far from being untrue, myths are the best way— sometimes the only way— of conveying truths that would otherwise remain inexpressible. We have come from God, Tolkien argued, and inevitably the myths woven by us, though they do contain error, still reflect a splintered fragment of the true light, the eternal truth that is with God. Myths may be misguided, but they steer however shakily toward the true harbor.[12]

The Bible follows a plotline that stories ever since love to copy: Creation, Fall, Rescue, and Restoration. Take for instance the "kill the dragon; get the girl" plotline. Jesus said a reason He came was to defeat the works of the devil. And, one day He will present the church, the bride of Christ, to His Father at the wedding feast of the Lamb.

Kill the dragon; get the girl.

I have shown this to students and seen them go to movies with friends, after which they used the storyline of the movie to explain the story of the gospel. Again, we seek to have gospel conversations that start in the worldview of the unbeliever and take them to the cross. This is a helpful way for students to see.

While this has become very helpful, the approach I mentioned called the "3 Circles" has become a favorite not only for me to share it but also as a way to teach students. This approach to sharing Christ explains the metanarrative mentioned above, but does so in a way a student (or you) can sketch out on a napkin in a coffee shop. I have done so myself in fact.

Take a sheet of paper and imagine you are talking with a teenager or a parent. As you converse about life, about issues they face, about passion or pain, draw a circle in the upper left corner. In the circle write the word "God's Design." (See Picture 1) Explain how God made a beautiful world, how our desire for happiness, our sense of purpose, our aversion to pain come from God's hardwiring us in His image.

Then, ask the person if they see ways in which things have gone in our world. Perhaps share things from your own experience. Note how our world is filled with broken relationships, broken hearts, and broken dreams. As you talk about this, draw a circle in the top right corner. Write the word "brokenness" in it.

Converse with the person about examples of brokenness. Draw an arrow from the first circle to the second, and write the word "Sin" over the arrow, explaining how sin came into the world and led to the brokenness we see all around us. Draw some curvy arrows (see diagram) extending from the Brokenness circle.

Picture 1

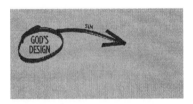

(See Picture 2) Explain how we tend to try and fix the brokenness in our lives by ourselves through our good works, our own ideas of religion, or running from it through denial.

Picture 2

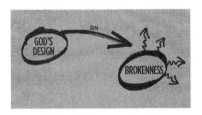

Then draw a circle in the center toward the bottom. Write the word "Gospel" in it. Describe how Jesus came to bring good news, which is what gospel means. Explain His death for our sin and His resurrection and, perhaps, share your own story of how Jesus changed you. Draw an arrow from the circle of Brokenness to the Gospel circle. Write the words "Repent" and "Believe" on each side of the arrow. (See Picture 3) Explain how Jesus did everything necessary for us to be forgiven for our sin and rescued from ourselves; we simply come to God in repentance and faith.

Picture 3

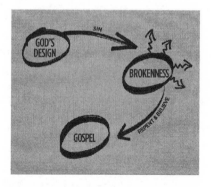

Finally, draw an arrow from Gospel to God's Design. Write the words "Pursue" and "Recover" on each side of it. (See Picture 4) Explain how that once we meet the Lord we can live our lives in pursuit of God, growing in our knowledge of Him and in our understanding of His purpose in our lives, until we ultimately experience the beauty of the place God has designed for us forever in heaven.

You can see videos of this conversation guide explained by Pastor Jimmy Scroggins at http://www.namb.net/namb1cb2col.aspx?id=12884910636 and by Alvin Reid at http://multimedia.sebts.edu/?p=5593.

Try this: Give students a sheet of paper and a pen one week. Show them on a marker board how to share Christ using the 3 circles. Have them draw it with you. Then, pair them up and have one student share this with another. Challenge them to do the same with a friend at school that week on a sheet of paper or a napkin.

Picture 4

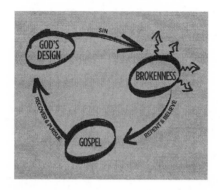

Try this: Check out *The Story* and *Life on Mission* in the App store for your smart phone.

While we want to help students (and ourselves) share Christ in the course of daily life, we also will want to create times to help students engage their campuses for Christ. A vital way to do this is through involvement with Christian club such as FCA. Michael Wood, now senior pastor at First Baptist Church, West Monroe, Louisiana (think Duck Dynasty), previously served for years as student pastor there. Here are some ways he led his ministry to engage their schools.

Notice in this list his priority of helping the FCA or other clubs:[13]

- *I placed HIGH importance on being on campus and a part of school groups. Our staff rotated schools lunches and tried to hit our main schools at least once a week.*

- *We found creative ways to serve kids and teachers. The normal draw is the football teams, cheerleaders, etc., but there are a huge variety of groups in the schools that can be used.*

- *For things like FCA, we told the sponsors that the answer was always, "yes." There would be times they would contact us late, late the night before or early that morning because a speaker had dropped. We were always there when they needed us!*

- *One unique thing that John (Avant, their former pastor) helped establish here is that for West Monroe High School, we have lined up mentors for every player and trainer.*

- *We gave out tons of POPSICLES! Even at times traveling to where school groups were having their training camps out of town to bless them.*

- *One of the neat things that I saw here was giving students permission to serve their own campus. We had one group of seniors do a Senior Serve Day instead of a Senior Prank. They split their group into two smaller groups. The first group actually served lunch and cleaned the lunchroom for the cafeteria ladies. The other group organized, set-up, and served an appreciation lunch for the cafeteria ladies in the library during the lunchtime. The students had the idea, planned, and implemented the entire thing. Needless to say, it made my heart full.*

- *The two most important people at the school to have a good relationship with: principle and receptionist at the front desk. Bless them with goodies.*

- *Chaplains are a great way to be around students. (And not just for the football team!) Guy's teams, girl's teams, large or small.*

- *One idea: When it comes time for standardize testing in the schools, ask the leadership if you can do like a quiz game show at lunch with questions that prep them for their testing. Give away candy, drinks, or whatever. It gets you in*

*front of students and is a help to the adminis-
tration and students.*

As you can see, they focused on serving and helping the school. We hope you have figured out this as a theme of the book by now! In order to have opportunities to share Christ, we have to demonstrate our care for the schools.

Josh Glidewell, student pastor at Living Hope Church in the Memphis area has involved parents with his students in weekly outreach on Wednesday nights. He also involves students and parents in a new church plant.[14] He writes:

*We partner with our church plant in
Midtown Memphis to facilitate a Gospel Centered program. Our students work alongside
parents and other volunteers to teach students
from the neighborhood the gospel through
Bible stories, worship and crafts. While this is
mostly student led, we encourage our parents
to come along side of these students to encourage and support them in this ministry. This has
been largely successful for us as we try to create
a missional culture not just in our students, but
in our parents as well.*

Finally, Jeff Borton at Christ Fellowship Church, Miami, takes his students on a mission trip to their city every year. Miami is a mission field, after all! I had the honor of speaking at this experience recently. Students get up early, serve their community, and share Christ all day, and then gather for incredible worship in the evening. I even got to speak on South Beach one night. These students become immersed in the mission for a week and then are reminded every week to be on mission in their schools and neighborhoods.

If we can get students to love God and love people to the point that they live their lives on mission, we can see a vibrant student ministry emerge, and we might see revival as well.

Food for Thought

- As you get out into your community, how do you also equip your students to be active in sharing their faith in their schools?
- What could you do in the coming year to help your students to see the world from the vision of a missionary and live like missionaries on their campuses?
- How much consistent attention do you give to stress to your students the importance of loving God and loving people, of fulfilling both

the Great Commandment and the Great Commission?

CHAPTER 5

GET REAL:
Real Impact for a Real World

"Never believe that a few caring people can't change the world. For, indeed, that's all who ever have."

— Margaret Mead

We have a phenomenal coffee house in the Raleigh-Durham area called Sola. It serves Counter Culture Coffee, stays full of patrons from every walk of life and age group imaginable, and has enjoyed great success in our area. In fact, our final edit of this book is happening in its aromatic walls (it's really crowded and full of life!). It's owned by a former student at

Southeastern Seminary, a man named John who started the business not as a "Christian Coffee House," but as an extremely fine Third Place where the gospel can flourish out of ordinary relationships.

We've been talking about impacting the public schools primarily as they offer such a vital mission field. But what is the long-term goal of all this? Certainly the goal is first to make disciples of students who will walk with Jesus their whole lives and be disciple-makers themselves. And, we hope student pastors, parents, adult workers, and students who know Jesus will be encouraged to live on mission. But there is another related goal that is more long term in nature: we want students to be so aware of the gospel's power that in their adult lives, no matter their location or vocation, they continue to live missionally for Jesus, like my friend John and his coffee house. In order for students to "get this" in the long term, they need to be engaged in the mission now. While we have focused on public schools, we also want to impact students in Christian schools as well as the growing home school population.

Recovering a Book of Acts Vision

In the book of Acts what you read about is what some call "total evangelism," or simply, to quote Leighton Ford, the total participation of all believers in the task in the total proclamation of the gospel to all unbelievers. That's an old school way of saying everyone who knew Jesus seemed to be burdened to help everyone who does not know Jesus to hear the gospel.

> Where you live does not make you a missionary; the mission you're on makes you a missionary.

In Acts they showed and shared Christ. Michael Green in his book *Evangelism in the Early Church* says this basic approach continued for decades after the first century as Christianity spread in a far more hostile environment than ours today. It's easy for Christian students in public schools to be intimidated by the vast numbers of unbelievers and the growing wickedness apparent in so many schools. Encourage them by reminding how God took a very small band of believers, a den of disciples, to change the whole world. Green remarks:

It was a small group of eleven men whom Jesus commissioned to carry on his work, and bring the gospel to the whole world. They were not distinguished; they were not well educated; they had no influential backers ... If they had stopped to weigh up the probabilities of succeeding in their mission, even granted their conviction that Jesus was alive, and that his Spirit went with them to equip them for their task, their hearts must surely have sunk, so heavily were the odds weighed against them. How could they possibly succeed? And yet they did.[15]

As you get out personally and involve your student ministry in getting out into the culture, it may help to go back through the book of Acts to see how the early church spread the good news. How did they show Christ and share Christ? They not only spoke about Jesus; they put the gospel on display by how they lived. Here are a few ways they displayed the gospel as they also spoke the message in Acts:

- They all spoke of the mighty works of God (2:10-11)
- They had preachers like Peter who stood up and spoke to crowds (2:14-40)
- They saw signs and wonders (2:43)

- They demonstrated remarkable concern for the needy (2:44-45; 4:32-37)
- They shared boldly in the face of persecution (4:1-20)
- They cared for the outcasts of society (the lame man in chapter 3, Samaria in chapter 8)
- They demonstrated an unwavering commitment to truth (4:20)
- They prayed fervently and together (4:23-31)

Here is the good news: young people today can display the gospel the same way! God still answers prayer and does remarkable things through His children. He honors boldness, compassion, conviction, and answers the prayers of His children. Central to the gospel advance in Acts was the place of *relationships* and *community*. The early Christians loved one another and outsiders, and demonstrated a community worth belonging to. Brian Mills recognizes it's easier to sit in the office and plan events than to do the hard work of relationship building, but he also notes the benefit of paying that price:

> *The key to student ministry is found in building relationships, not in athletics or any key ability. If you can build relationships you can be effective. I once put a young white guy*

from the suburbs in an inner city ministry in Nashville. People said he didn't fit, that it wouldn't work. Maybe he was not from the 'hood, but he could build relationships. He got senior adults to make PBJ sandwiches for the ball teams. He went to their games. Guess who didn't go to their games? Their dads. A young guy about 21 from the 'burbs became like a dad to these young men.

The players do not care if you know about football; they care if you care about them. The key to ministry is to maximize the relationships you build.

A Missionary Regardless of Vocation or Location

For a while there was a great commercial shown on college football Saturdays in the fall. The commercial showed a variety of student athletes who "went pro" in all sorts of professions other than sports. The point: every student athlete's goal is to become a professional; but only a few will be professional athletes. In the same way, the vast majority of students we reach for Christ will not be pastors or missionaries in the sense of going out as part of a mission's agency. But every single person who is breathing and knows Christ is a missionary. Where you live and what you do for a living do not make you a missionary; the mission you are on makes you one. It may be the most remarkable thing you do in your ministry is to help young people catch a vision for living missionally regardless of their career.

Raising Up Missionaries in Christian Schools and Among Home Schoolers

This book has focused on the great mission field of the public school campus. But what about Christian and home school children in your ministry? Josh attended public school for part of his education but graduated from a large Christian school. His sister Hannah attended private school but graduated from a large public school in our area. I have yet to find a Christian school that has an undoubtedly 100% saved student body. There are plenty of cultural, superficial folks in the Christian school, but there are also young people on fire for the Lord. Helping them to learn to share Christ matters as much as reaching the public schools.

If you are breathing, and you know Jesus, you are a missionary.

Here are some ideas for involving home school and private school students:

- *Encourage these students to be involved in any outreach you do related to the public school.* Tail gate parties, providing meals for teams, and other opportunities outside the normal class time offer ways students can help. And, if you provide a meal on Friday afternoons for football teams, for instance, home schoolers have a more flexible schedule to help with preparation.

- *Encourage them to be active sharing Christ via social media* (see below).

- *Encourage home school families to do mission trips as a family, including mission projects in their neighborhood.*

- *If possible, leverage influence in the Christian school to be more active in mission work in your area and via mission trips.*

I have talked with more than a few student pastors who struggle with home school families focused more on protecting their children (and often overprotecting them) than on advancing the gospel. How do you overcome this? One way is to offer examples of home school families--and I have met more than a few of them--who take the mission of God seriously as a family. Like Morgan and Brianna's families. These young ladies and a few other friends started a ministry while in middle school that has raised over $50,000 to build a safe house in Moldova. They have been there several times in their teen years, and Morgan's entire family went one year. Brianna is now a student at our college. Both Morgan and Brianna come from home school families, as do all the ladies except one, breaking the stereotype--often earned--that home schooling can blunt the spear of gospel advance. In *As You Go* Morgan shared about their ministry:

> *Learning to dig through the Word with godly girls was an invaluable means in my life of growing closer to God. I'm so grateful for the investment that my mom and several other ladies made in our lives then to shape us into the teens that we are becoming now. Through a variety of circumstances—our church's first Global Impact Conference, a trip to India at age thirteen, and others—God continued to show me the needs of the world. The Fourth of July, 2010, happened to be on a Sunday. In Bible Fellowship that morning my eighth grade girls' class spent time praying and thanking God for our freedom. At one point I mentioned the fact that I was grateful for not being literally*

enslaved in physical bondage, specifically enslaved to satisfying the sexual desires of ruthless men. I mentioned my concern for trafficked girls. A few days later, a few friends and I decided to have a sleepover. We shared about how we really wanted to do something with our high school years bigger than ourselves—something to make a difference. We began to focus on the issue of trafficked women, and the ministry of Save Our Sisters (SOS) was born. Since the birth of SOS, the Lord has blessed us with over $50,000 to set the captives free! God has been continually shaping the vision and goal of our ministry. The following July my fellow SOS member Brianna and I were able to travel to Cahul, Moldova, often described as the engine of the sex slave trade. With a population of only 5 million, nearly 25 percent of all Moldovan women are trafficked throughout Europe. Women serve as Moldova's number one export. During our time in Moldova, we visited a Freedom Home in the capital city of Chisnau for rescued victims of trafficking. From our first greetings with the girls, we immediately felt the love of Christ exude from their sweet spirits. These women are living out redemption stories every day. We learned that over the past ten years, 30,000 women have been trafficked from the city of Cahul. As a ministry, SOS began pursuing the dream of building a safe home in

Cahul. We are working to make this dream a reality. To help us achieve this goal, we work with Immanuel Baptist Church in Cahul, a young church planted by Christ Baptist Church in Raleigh, North Carolina.In addition to the home, land in Cahul will also be used for an orphanage and sports camp. Sports camps serve as the main means of evangelism in the lives of Moldovan teens. Through this sports camp, we will take steps toward the prevention of trafficking. By teaching the girls the telltale signs of traffickers, potential victimization can be avoided. As for the orphanage, that will be a preventative step as well. By housing orphan children, the girls will be off the streets and minimize their vulnerability. Children of the orphanage and sports camp will hear the good news of the gospel and will prayerfully begin to root themselves in the love of Christ. Experiencing freedom in Christ is the most effective means of prevention, intervention, and restoration for the whole scope of the human trafficking industry. We praise God for such an awesome opportunity to serve in multiple capacities!

Give Your Students a Vision

We believe young adults like these exist in every student ministry. They need a *vision* for gospel impact through their lives, *encouragement* to live for Jesus, and *permission* to do so while young.

Student pastor Josh Evans has found some ways to do this through his ministry at Union Grove Baptist Church in North Carolina.[16] One of the things I love about what he says involves his taking traditional events like a youth DiscipleNow and turning it to be more about gospel advance.

> *We have done a few things regarding engaging students and the community that have worked really well and have been big "wins" for our student ministry.*
>
> 1. *Basketball–like many churches we have a gym. I have utilized this to reach students in our local public school system. I open the gym after youth group and stay for several hours for the students to play ball. We had several start coming from the public school, and it has grown and grown. For instance, I have probably met like 40 new students through this program, and had the privilege to connect with them over the past 8 months. I have received many more inroads into the public school system through this ministry.*

2. *Love our City–One thing we have done with the students in our ministry is a yearly event entitled "love our city." I have taken the concepts of a DNOW and a community outreach event, and have combined them. It is a 2-day event. We kick off the weekend with a worship service. Then, we break into groups and head out to different work projects (homeless shelters, rescue mission, addiction facilities, shut-ins in our church, pregnancy care centers, the local public school, and more). We serve at these locations throughout the day. Then, we have a worship service with games to follow. Then, the students head to families homes for the night. We get up the next day and serve some more and then end with a service and an activity. This is one of our highest attended events of the year, because students in this generation want to be a part of something bigger than them.*

I love that last line: "students in this generation want to be part of something bigger than them." This certainly marks the Millennial generation. Challenge your students to something God-sized, like the gospel.

Your involvement with students in the mission does not have to involve some massive effort requiring significant funds. Kris Kuriger, student pastor at Hagood Memorial Baptist Church in South Carolina offers examples of simple acts of kindness they do as a ministry. You can involve public, private, and home school youth in these:[17]

Here are a couple of ways our student ministry has been missional in the schools. First, we try to do an event in the schools once a month both to build relationships with lost students and to bless the teachers and administration. These include teacher breakfasts, lunch Bible studies, etc. Second, we serve by painting classrooms, picking up trash around campus, and staying after football games to pick up trash.

My friend at Liberty University, David Wheeler, has said that if you are unwilling to pick up trash to serve others, you probably wouldn't wash feet like Jesus, either.

Student pastor Marty Middleton in Apex, North Carolina, has focused on a few specific ways to get out:[18]

> 1. *Each Friday in the fall, we feed the varsity football team at Middle Creek High School (Mustangs), which is only*

about 5 minutes from the church. We have several students who attend there. Several folks from Fairview prepare the meals each week, and help serve. We have been able to build a great relationship with some of the football parents who come help serve the meal as well.

2. *Each year, we have a Mustang Sunday at church, and invite the team and their families. It's been a great connecting point, with many relationships being built and seeds of the gospel being planted.*

3. *I substitute at Middle Creek several times a month, on my day off from my church job. When I moved to this area, I tried to go have lunch with students. In our case, the list of hoops to jump through to get to do this (understandably, for security reasons, I get that) made me see that, since I had a teaching degree, subbing was more effective. I have connected with many students this way, some of which have come to know the Lord, and started coming to Fairview.*

4. *Over the past couple years, I have been able to meet for a deeper level of discipleship with a few guys outside the*

church. I usually choose 3-4 guys to do this on a weekly basis. We read books like "Don't Waste Your Life", "Do Hard Things", and study the Bible.

Take a Mission Trip to the Internet

One of the ways you can help students make an impact for the gospel is through helping them to take a mission trip to the Internet. Students spend a lot of time online in the world of Facebook, Twitter, Instagram, Pinterest, Tumblr, and so on. You can leverage their impact online through a couple of ways. One, help them to see that world as a viable mission field. In *As You Go* I (Alvin) noted three places student ministries should seek to engage their students in gospel advance, through solid, evangelistic mission trips to:

The nations. Take a trip annually, or if that is too much for where your ministry is currently, every other year. Josh took over 40 students to Puerto Rico this past summer. While not technically another country, it certainly offered a ministry outside the context his students live in daily. We believe one of the best things you can do for students and their parents is to help them see the value of getting out of the country on mission before they finish high school. Creating ways to help students and families do this matters.

Cities. If we reach the cities of America we can reach the whole world. Perhaps a mission trip overseas annually is too much for your student ministry. Go out of the country one year and to a major U.S. city the next. Expose your students to gospel ministry outside their normal context.

Your own area. Many churches increasingly take a mission trip to their own area for a week or more annually. The church I (Alvin) serve part time and the church Josh grew in as a youth––Richland Creek Community Church just north of Raleigh––has an annual "trip" to our community called Live. Love. Serve. Last year ours included a free medical and dental clinic, a free pizza dinner one night (note: we do several of these annually, and our last one had over 2000 people attend), and a food drive that collected 38,000 pounds of food for the local food ministry in our area. Setting aside a week to be focused on mission in our area can help to create an ongoing "get out" mentality.

While these three matter a great deal, we now have a new, fourth mission field, that of social media. We recently had a "30 Days of Going" emphasis on Southeastern Seminary's campus where many students and faculty committed to attempting to share Christ every day for the 30 days of September. In addition to many testimonies of students doing outreach in our city, going on visits for their churches, and talking to co-workers, servers, and others as they go through their day, some have used the Internet and social media well.

Kiersten is in my college class. She posted a status update on Facebook about The Story and its beautiful way of sharing Christ. She added that anyone interested in hearing more could message her. She had an old friend message her, allowing her to share Christ with him.

There was a time centuries ago when maps centered on rivers, as they represented the primary means of travel and where cities were established. More recently, roads form the heart of our maps, although maps with airplane hubs and routes matter as well. But today, the world of social media has shrunk the world, allowing us to travel anywhere with a click to talk to people from all over the world. Last week a student who uses The Story app from Spread Truth showed me how in just one weekend he had people look at the Story presentation of the gospel from across the U.S. and two other continents.

I have met numerous young people in recent years that have led friends to Christ while chatting online. Believers have always used social networks of their time to spread the good news of Jesus. Paul used the networks of the synagogue, the marketplace, and places of public debate like Mars Hill. Martin Luther nailing the 95 Theses on a church door represented a normal way of communicating in his time; John Wesley used the Society structure of his day to organize a great revival; evangelist D.L. Moody used massive urban meeting to preach the gospel in a time of rising cities in the Industrial Revolution. Today, social media offers a tremendous way to help students reach out.

Here are a few ways students can be encouraged to get out through social media.

- *Get them at the same time to post their testimony as a Facebook note or on their blog or Tumblr, and link to that with Twitter or status updates.* Or, send a message to friends and ask them to read it and give their feedback.
- *Tweet or post key verses, maybe a series noting the narrative of the gospel.*
- *Tweet/post on Instagram links to places like viewthestory.com, iamsecond.com, or other sites*

that share Christ. You can create some tweets as examples to help them.

- *Set aside an hour a week online just for the gospel*, like "virtual visitation" where they take that time to talk to a friend about Christ.[19]

Try this: Gather some of your sharpest (and most savvy on social media) students as a "think tank" to dream some ways to make an impact though social media. They may come up with better ideas than we could!

Create a Culture of Service

Let's face it: the youth years can become narcissistic, and too many adults treat students like they are the center of the universe. Getting a servanthood culture in your ministry will help students grow in grace and will open doors to share Christ. They will learn this as we live this. Wes Evans, current student pastor at First Baptist, Concord, in the Knoxville, Tennessee area offers a great example of this from his experience in a difficult area:[20]

When I was in St Louis the public schools were closed to youth pastors. Truly. I took the advice of Jimmy Scroggins, who trained me at Boyce College in Louisville: I found a need and met it. I served. My wife and I found out that the head football coach was painting the football field by himself late on Thursday nights before the game, like midnight late. We asked if we could do it so he could go home to be with his family (you know how much they work in the fall especially!). He trained us one week and the job was ours. From that one act of service, we were invited to many opportunities to serve on this public school campus in very public ways. It began a relationship with the head football coach and the principal at the high school that brought benefits for years to come. The first came when they called me from a conference meeting and asked me on speakerphone if I would do them a favor and start a Bible study at the school "like an FCA group." I said yes immediately. They later asked my wife to help coach a team even though it was against their policy to let non-faculty members coach. They cut red tape with us in several ways, because of one act of service.

Helping your students to see where opportunities to serve exist and jumping on those can offer surprising benefits. Whether your ministry has only public school students or represents a mixture of public, private, and home school youth, creating a culture of service will help students to show and to share the gospel and see God at work. This can carry with them the rest of their lives.

The First Baptist Church of West Monroe has developed a more involved example of outreach through service. The West Monroe High School football team has national prominence, including being featured on ESPN in a series in recent years. The church developed a mentorship program with the students. In summary, this is what has happened:[21]

First Baptist Church of West Monroe has provided this program to the West Monroe High School football team for about 5 years. The goal is to connect strong, godly men with each high school football player, no matter his position or frequency on the field. If the player's name is on the roster, he has a mentor. The responsibility of the mentor is to stay connected to his assigned player-through whatever avenue works best between the two of them. Examples might be through phone calls/texts, dinner out once in a while, etc. The mentor is to do his best to attend as many football games during the season as possible, and to follow up with the player after those games. Prayer requests are shared, and the mentor does his best to also stay in touch with the parents; or at least meet them at the beginning of the season. If there are any concerns regarding the players, the mentor is responsible to report those to the team chaplain.

We begin each season with a special introductory supper for the players and mentors to meet each other. This is shared over pizza, and normally held at either our church or another participating church. We also introduce a book that is strongly encouraged to be read by the players and mentors, which also becomes the "theme" for the year. These books are donated by a member of First West, in honor of their son who was killed in a car accident in the past.

The program is open to any local church in the West Monroe area that provides us with names of mentors. We then contact those churches each year to help us find mentors. There is a bit of hard work that goes into pairing up each player. Some men request more than one player; some request repeat players, etc. This is done before the introductory supper, with flexibility of making changes.

Food for Thought

- Do you have students in home school or private school settings? How might you get them involved in reaching out?

- Is one of your core values of your ministry to get students on missions trips including trips outside the country? Why or why not?

- What is the vision your most active students have to live on mission for Jesus?

CONCLUSION
What Getting Out Looks Like

Brian Mills, quoted several times in this book already, served as student pastor at Long Hollow Baptist Church near Nashville, Tennessee and Second Baptist Church, Houston, Texas, before taking his recent role at the Englewood Baptist Church in Jackson, Tennessee. He has tremendous wisdom and experience in the area of getting out. He summarizes well what we have sought to tell you:

> *Campus ministry done in a sporadic way always equals failure. Many student pastors have the issue of more schools to cover than they can humanly accomplish, so they spread themselves too thin: "I am going to hit 25 schools in a month," they say. You will not succeed doing this. A great challenge is how to impact all the campuses. Jeff Lovingood taught me to focus on those you can guarantee to reach every week. Don't be a high five youth pastor who is at a lot of places but knows no one; be a relational youth pastor. You can't do that hitting 3 games*

in a night. When I was a youth pastor without any help, I picked two schools and stuck to those, and occasionally went to one other.

Relational ministry is the hardest ministry. It's easy to sit in the office and not build relationships. You may have to make some hard decisions to create time to be on campuses.

In my first seven weeks in Jackson, I had already met with the administrators of the key schools in our area. I start with the top in the administration because I want their favor. You do not want them to think you are sneaking in the back door. If they get a hint of that you are done at that school. The most important person is the principal, after that it is the receptionist/ principal's assistant. They always love Chick Fil a cookies! If they don't want you in, they can stop you there.

After these, I seek to get to know coaches and those related to sports, which includes the band director. All teams, all groups matter. I take freezer pops to all the practices, band practice, etc. Everyone gets a freezer pop!

How has this worked? In Jackson, seven weeks ago we had 90 youth. We started effective student ministry getting into the community. We had 400 attending in seven weeks.

Now, Brian has years of experience and a team to help, but even with that the result in seven weeks is remarkable. You may not have that trajectory, but you can see growth as you get out.

Pastors: Let Your Student Pastor Go

I (Alvin) spend a lot of time both with lead pastors and student pastors. I want to humbly offer a word of counsel primarily to pastors regarding a frustration I hear constantly from student pastors. It has to do with two words that have become a staple of the institutional church that would have been unknown in the early church before a time when buildings dominated church life. The two words?

Office hours.

I recognize the student pastors I hang out and interact with have probably a more evangelistic bent to them. I am unambiguously committed to the fact that ministers of the gospel––regardless of title––should give much time to sharing Christ themselves and to helping believers live the mission. But the student pastors I know have perhaps no greater frustration than the fact that they have an expectation to be at the church building "x" hours a week when they would much rather be in the local schools, at ball games, and in other ways interacting with students in the community.

Pastors, you have every right to expect student pastors to work hard and to have hours where they are available to lead, plan, witness, disciple, and mentor. Just please do one thing: let student pastors fill some of those hours off the church campus. In other words, let your student pastor go. Don't fire them; just free them. It seems a bit silly to say with our words how vital it is for the people we lead to live missional lives when we actually structure our church ministry leaders' assignments to spend most of their time in the church building. If you are a student pastor, you need accountability. Unfortunately, more than a few of your peers could use a little shot of discipline in the arm and you suffer for it. If you feel the need to be out of the church building and in the schools and the community more, help your pastor to see that you are not shirking your responsibility to be available to others, but for you "office hours" can be held away from the church campus. The most vibrant student ministries I know feature student pastors who spend as much time on the public school campus each week as on the church campus.

How much time do you need to spend in the office? It depends on a lot of factors. Counseling is best done there, as is meeting with other staff or time with leaders planning events. Some student pastors are quite effective in getting loads of students to come and hang out at their office after school. But from what I see and hear, most student pastors (and I daresay other ministers) spend way too much time filling office hours in the church and not enough time being in the community. This is a remarkably modern phenomenon created more by the industrial revolution and the rise of corporate America than the mission of God or the needs of a broken world. We live in a Third Place world where even corporate America increasingly encourages workers to be portable, to work from home, in Starbucks, in virtual offices. Over the last decade the number of people working away from the office via the Internet has grown from 10 million to 28 million. Maybe once again the church can relearn ministry in the community.

Pastor, talk to your student pastor. Student pastor, talk to your pastor. Staff, get together and talk about your mission and how you communicate it, because how you structure your ministry daily says more to those you lead than what you say with your words.

The "get out" mindset need not be relegated to student ministry only. Figure out a way to help the person given primary responsibility to work with students to actually be with students more during the week. Ask yourself if the expectations of staff in terms of office hours and schedule really reflect a robust commitment to the Great Commission. If you have a student pastor with a zeal for witnessing to lost students, to mentoring growing students, and to helping saved students live as missionaries, set him free to be in the community more than a cubicle. Let your student pastor go!

APPENDIX
Best Practices

Here's what we want you to get: the answer to reaching students and their families in your area is not fundamentally tied to getting the best evangelism program or best evangelist to preach in your town. It is 1) to develop a life of prayer and a depth of gospel insight that helps you see the community through Jesus' eyes; 2) a refocusing of ministry outside the church building, and then 3) everyday people (including you and your students!) doing everyday things with gospel intentionality.

Review all the real examples from real student pastors offered throughout the book. Jeremy Lewis serves as student pastor at the Central Baptist Church in College Station, Texas. He offers an excellent summary of the examples we have been sharing:[22]

- Meet the principals

- Pray for principals and leaders and let them know you are praying
- Connect with coaches
- Know the rules and follow them
- Serve the school
- Partner with organizations like FCA
- Go to lunch on campus (if possible)
- Make your staff's presence known at events
- Don't be afraid to introduce yourself to students
- Challenge your students to introduce their friends to the staff when they are on campus.

In addition, here are a few more ideas scattered throughout the book:

- Prepare your sermons to students at Starbucks or another Third Place, around people not in your church.
- Look for a new way to serve your school; if you have several schools, reach out to a new one.
- If schools have been closed, take principles from this book and make one more effort to get connected with your local public school.

- Mentor a handful of hungry students to have Great Commission conviction.
- Mentor a struggling student with his classwork as a way to connect with a school.
- Involve your students in your work of getting out.

ENDNOTES

1   Cited in Tim Chester and Steve Timmis, *Everyday Church: Gospel Communities on Mission* (Crossway, Re:Lit: 2013) Kindle Edition, 14.

2   Chester and Timmis, *Everyday Church*, 10. Italics added.

3   Email from Spencer Barnard to the Author, May 1, 2014.

4   Brian Mills, interview via Skype, October 2, 2014.

5   http://everyschool.com/a-youth-ministry-is-campus-ministry. Accessed September 30 2014.

6   Hugh Halter and Matt Smay, *The Tangible Kingdom: Creating Incarnational Community* (San Francisco: Josey-Bass, 2008). Cited in https://scottemery.wordpress.com/category/church-stuff/page/6/.

7   http://twloha.com/vision/story. Accessed April 9, 2010.

8   Mike Camire, Email to Author, May 7, 2013.

9   Matthew Sawyer, Email to Author, December 4, 2013.

10 Jason Engle, Email to Author, December 2, 2013.

11 Mark Senter, *When God Shows Up: A History of Protestant Youth Ministry in America* (Grand Rapids: Baker Academic, 2010), Kindle Locations 845-856.

12 Eric Geiger, Matt Chandler, and Josh Patterson (2012-09-05). *Creature of the Word: The Jesus-Centered Church* (p. 84). B&H Publishing Group. Kindle Edition.

13 Email from Micheal Wood to Alvin L. Reid August 27, 2014.

14 Email from Joshua Glidewell to Author, September 22, 2014.

15 Michael Green, *Evangelism in the Early Church* (Grand Rapids: Eerdmans, 1970), 13.

16   Email from Josh Evans to Author, December 20, 2013.

17   Email from Kris Kuriger to Author, November 30, 2013.

18   Email from Marty Middleton to Author, November 30, 2013.

19   Adapted from *As You Go,* p. 179.

20   Wes Evans, Email to Author, April 4, 2014.

21   Kelli DeBord, Email to Author, September 23, 2014.

22   Jeremy Lewis, Email to Author, February 24, 2013.

Made in the USA
San Bernardino, CA
09 September 2016